# Mrs. Paine's Garage

PANTHEON BOOKS
60 YEARS OF PUBLISHING

Also by Thomas Mallon

# Mrs. Paine's Garage

and

the Murder of John F. Kennedy

## Thomas Mallon

Pantheon Books, New York

*PAINE*

Permissions acknowledgments are on page 211.

Library of Congress Cataloging-in-Publication Data

Mallon, Thomas, 1951–
Mrs. Paine's garage: and the murder of
John F. Kennedy / Thomas Mallon.
ISBN 0-375-42117-3
1. Paine, Ruth. 2. Oswald, Lee Harvey—Friends and associates.
3. Porter, Marina Oswald—Friends and associates. 4. Kennedy,
John F. (John Fitzgerald), 1917–1963—Assassination.
5. Irving (Tex.)—Biography. I. Title.

E842.9 .M279 2002 364.1'524'092—dc21 [B] 2001036157
www.pantheonbooks.com

*Book design by M. Kristen Bearse*

Printed in the United States of America
First Edition
2 4 6 8 9 7 5 3 1

for Dan Frank
with lasting thanks and affection

AFFIDAVIT IN ANY FACT

THE STATE OF TEXAS
COUNTY OF DALLAS

BEFORE ME, PATSY COLLINS, a Notary Public in and for said County, State of Texas, on this day personally appeared RUTH HYDE PAINE/W/F/31, 2515 W. FIFTH STREET, IRVING, TEXAS. Who, after being by me duly sworn, on oath deposes and says:

I have lived at the above address for about 4 years. My husband, Michael and I had been separated for about a year. In the early winter of 1963, I went to a party in Dallas because I heard that some people would be there that spoke Russian. I was interested in the language. At that party I met Lee Oswald and his Russian wife Marina. About a month later I went to visit them on Neely Street. In May I asked her to stay with me because Lee went to New Orleans to look for work. About two weeks later I took Marina to New Orleans to join her husband. Around the end of September I stopped by to see them while I was on vacation. I brought Marina back with me to Irving. He came in 2 weeks, later, but did not stay with his wife and me. Marina's husband would come and spend most of the weekends with his wife. Through my neighbor, we heard there was an opening at the Texas School Book Depository. Lee applied and was accepted. Lee did not spend last weekend there. He came in about 5 pm yesterday and spent the night. I was asleep this morning when he left for work.

RUTH HYDE PAINE

SUBSCRIBED AND SWORN TO BEFORE ME THIS 22 DAY OF November A. D., 1963.

PATSY COLLINS
Notary Public, Dallas County, Texas

# Contents

# Acknowledgments

I am grateful, of course and above all, to Ruth Hyde Paine for her unfailing and sometimes stressful cooperation in recollecting the events of 1963 and other periods of her life.

Michael Paine, Marin Paine, Priscilla Johnson McMillan, Raymond Entenmann, Ruth Carter Stevenson, and John McAdams all provided interviews and important assistance.

I am indebted to Steven Tilley and Matthew Fulgham of the National Archives and Records Administration; Patricia O'Donnell of the Friends Historical Library at Swarthmore College; Paula Stewart of the Amon Carter Museum; Lisa Pena of the Mary Couts Burnett Library (Texas Christian University); and the staff of the Irving, Texas, Public Library.

I would like to thank the John Simon Guggenheim Foundation for a grant in 2000–2001.

My agent, Mary Evans, provided deft assistance at a number of points; and I owe thanks to Andrea Barrett, Lucy Kaylin, Martin Beiser, and Fran Kiernan for reading the manuscript and offering suggestions.

Dan Frank—and Bill Bodenschatz—made this book possible.

Westport, Connecticut
August 12, 2001

Part One  November 21, 1963

# One

There would be bad news from Dallas tomorrow. But as 5:30 approached on this warm Thursday afternoon, Ruth Paine had little time to think about her pending divorce. As usual, she was in the midst of errands, driving her station wagon back from the supermarket with groceries for her own small, sundered family as well as the other oddly intact one that had been grafted onto it these last several months.

A copy of the divorce petition, which Ruth had filed eight days ago, was right now being postmarked near the offices of her lawyer in the Rio Grande National Building downtown. The dated facts in it—that she and Michael had been married on December 28, 1957, in Pennsylvania, and produced two children, Lynn (b. 1959) and Christopher (b. 1961), before separating "on or about September 1, 1962"—were more accurate than the supposed crux of the document, its declaration that her husband, now "the defendant," had "about six months before their said separation, commenced a course of unkind, harsh, cruel and tyrannical treatment . . . of such a nature as to render their further living together insupportable."

The legal boilerplate hardly described the painfully civilized breach between Ruth and Michael, or the temperate good will he showed whenever he now visited from his own apartment over in Grand Prairie. The two of them probably still saw more movies together than the average couple living under one roof. But the law was the law, and it required stern lies in the matter of divorce, even one arrived at as quietly as this.

Driving down Fifth Street, crossing Westbrook Drive, Ruth was surprised by a picture of domesticity that suddenly came into view. There, up ahead, under the oak tree on her own front lawn, stood Lee and Marina, playing with Junie in apparent contentment. The Oswalds, in contrast to the Paines, might bitch and bicker with each other much of the time—Lee had bawled out Marina over the phone just three nights ago—but their own separation was partial, temporary, and economic. Most nights Lee lived in a rooming house downtown, on North Beckley, closer to the book-warehouse job that Ruth had helped him get last month; Marina and Junie, and now four-week-old Rachel, stayed here with her in Irving, joined by their "Papa" on weekends, when the population of the four-room house would swell to seven. Ruth expected the situation to last until Christmas, perhaps a little longer, after which she would have to deal with missing Marina as she still dealt with missing Michael.

It was odd that Lee should be here tonight. He never came out before Friday, and never failed to call and ask permission before he made the trip. As soon as Ruth parked in the driveway—the garage was too full of the Paines' and the Oswalds' things to house the car—Marina came over to apologize for her husband's unexpected presence. "That's all right," Ruth answered, in Russian, the only language Marina spoke and the one in which Ruth herself, thanks to Marina's live-in presence, at last found herself becoming fluent.

Ruth also spoke Russian to Lee, and as he entered the house, on his way to the kitchen with some grocery bags, she greeted his helpful gesture with the news that had so many local people excited in one way or another.

*"Nahsh President Preyehdid y gorodoo."*

Almost forty years later, Ruth Paine remembers him responding with no more than an uninflected "Da," a sort of verbal shrug most accurately translated as "Uh, yeah." And yet, despite his evident indifference, she knows that Lee Oswald had understood her to say: "Our President is coming to town."

The small ranch house invited in all the late afternoon's light. The living room picture window, facing the street, went from the foundation to the roof, and from the kitchen Ruth could look out on the sunlight lowering itself upon the backyard, with its swing set and long clothesline, where she and Marina had hung so many diapers all fall. As Ruth went about preparing supper, she heard no signs of quarreling from Lee and Marina, either elsewhere in the house or out on the lawn—a relief, considering how harshly the young man had berated his wife three nights ago over the phone. The scolding had been prompted by a call Marina had asked Ruth to dial the night before that, Sunday, to WH 3-8993, the number of Lee's rooming house in Dallas. He'd given them the number himself, but now he wanted it stricken from Ruth's address book. Until they'd used it Sunday night, the two women hadn't known he was registered with his landlady as O. H. Lee, not Lee H. Oswald, the person Ruth had of course asked for.

Marina may have been upset by the incident, but she wasn't wholly surprised. Lee had these fantasies of being a great man, a big shot, she explained to Ruth; they drove him into foolish games like this one with the alias, when he should be sticking to

the hard business of being twenty-four years old with no higher
education or skills but a wife and two little girls to support.

Ruth hadn't pried into the explanation. Not because she lacked
grounds for suspicion of her friend's husband—for the past two
weeks she'd had a strong, particular reason to be wary—but out of
adherence to the standards of her character and adopted Quaker
religion. Lee, she knew, resented others' scrutiny, and Ruth was
no more likely to press him on private matters than she would be
to rummage through his possessions in her garage.

Tonight, as she finished getting supper on the table, Ruth remained unaware of the drama unfolding, out of earshot, between Lee and Marina. Without raising their voices, the couple
was struggling at the edge of a marital cliff. Before the sun was
down, Lee would ask his wife, three times, to consider leaving
Ruth's comfortable house and moving back together with him.
If Marina agreed, he would find them an apartment right away—
*tomorrow*, he promised. And he would get her a washing machine, just like the one she'd become accustomed to here in
Irving. But three times—by tomorrow night the number would
seem Biblical—Marina denied him his wish.

Tonight, Lee seemed to Ruth even more withdrawn than
usual. Of course, the matter of language, not so much a barrier
as a shaky bridge, always narrowed conversational possibilities.
Marina might be here, in part, to help Ruth with her Russian,
but Lee didn't want his wife learning English in return. He
claimed that this was so his own skills in the language—the
only lasting reward, aside from Marina, of his defection to the
USSR—wouldn't atrophy. But the truth was he liked Marina's

being isolated; dependent, albeit without much support, on him. So at the dinner table he continued speaking Russian to Ruth as well. "Effectively it reduced our conversations," she now explains, "which was okay with me, and I felt that's really how he wanted it, too. There wasn't much to say. I didn't want to get into any political stuff." The previous evening, she and Marina had talked of Christmas plans; Ruth had the idea of building a playhouse for the children, and it would be safer to return to that topic tonight than to speak of current events.

Ruth wished she could go into Dallas to watch the President's motorcade tomorrow morning. Three months ago, when visiting her sister in Washington, she had squandered a chance to hear Martin Luther King speak near the Lincoln Memorial. But even so, she knew it was better not to try getting a glimpse of John F. Kennedy. "I thought it would be fairly crowded. There always are questions of where do you park and how do you take care of the kids when you go in." So she and Marina would stay home, though even today, she says with a sigh: "I thought it would be nice to see him."

Once the dishes were done, Ruth still had to prepare a bottle for Chris, read him and Lynn a story, and get both children settled down for the night in the rear bedroom they shared with their mother. Lee and Marina were free to continue their negotiations in the front bedroom or the living room. Nine o'clock would arrive before Ruth was at last able to work on a much more modest project than the potential playhouse—lacquering some toy blocks she had made for the children. As soon as she entered her garage through the door connecting it to the dinette, its clutter came into view: someone had left the light on. The 100-watt overhead bulb threw the larger objects into relief against the white-painted walls. Ruth immediately got the feeling that Lee had been out here, probably just a little while ago, when she had been tending to the children. Marina—brought up frugally and, despite Ruth's attempts to make her feel at home, mindful of being a guest—always remembered to turn off the switch after coming for any of her things.

Ruth threaded her way through the jumble in search of the varnish. Along with Michael's drill press, some old tires, and a deepfreeze, whose top she would use for a work surface, the garage housed the table saw on which she had recently cut the blocks. Boxes with Lee and Marina's possessions rested between it and two chests of drawers; nearby was a blanket roll belonging to the Oswalds that Michael had had to move a couple of times when he came to work with his tools, as he still did on his visits.

Some of Ruth's own most personal possessions—letters and essays and private reflections—were stored in two metal file boxes out here in the garage. Among them was the senior paper she'd composed ten years ago at Antioch College. "I seek to fill the needs of those whom I meet," she had written;

> to give to the fullest of my ability to all who ask of me. I want to accept others, and to express this acceptance. Too many of the world's people go friendless through life, unable to share their deepest sorrows and joys with anyone. Too often we have not the time, or the inclination, to reach out to those who need help, to concern ourselves with their sorrows, to

care how the world is treating them. I seek to lead a life that
will never be so full of activities that I will be unable to take
time to meet the immediate needs of those around me.

Yesterday she had driven Marina to the dentist; today they'd
gotten Junie's TB-test results from the clinic. For months she
had taken care not to let her kindnesses to Marina appear a
usurpation of Lee's own role as provider, however intermit-
tently he filled it. She wanted him to know that she got as much
from Marina—the chance to hear and speak Russian, the companionship—as the other way around. Lee might be sullen and
suspicious (if someone asked Ruth, truthfulness would demand
the admission that she didn't much like him), but he was also
capable of small, sudden sympathies. On one recent weekend,
the subject of Ruth's divorce had come up between them. She'd
been "a little stunned" to hear him say, with a certain real feeling, that this must be a hard time for her.

Actually, without telling her, Lee disapproved of Michael
Paine's seeming indifference to his own family. Michael might
do a good job for them financially, but he left Ruth looking sad
whenever he breezed in and out for supper. He wasn't, Lee
thought, a good father; and so, after he finished playing with his
own girls tonight, Lee had made a point of playing with little
Chris Paine. The boy needed some extra attention from a man.
Marina had guessed the impulse behind this deed but said
nothing, lest she hurt Ruth's still-tender feelings for her husband. It would be one piece of information she had no guilt
about withholding.

Lee liked to stay up watching movies on TV, but tonight he

had gone to bed early. By the time Ruth finished with the blocks and stepped back into the house, only Marina was still up. The two women sat together on the couch, folding yet more laundry, and Marina told Ruth that Lee's unexpected presence tonight seemed motivated by a desire to patch up Monday night's telephone quarrel. Ruth asked for no further explanation, and Marina volunteered nothing more.

Sometime between eleven o'clock and eleven-thirty, before Marina retired to the front bedroom of this house that was never locked, the two young mothers said good night to each other. Ruth had not had an opportunity to say good night to Lee, but that was all right, since tomorrow was Friday, the start of the weekend, and she could expect to see him after he'd completed his day's work.

# Two

Like Lee Harvey Oswald, Ruth Hyde was the child of an insurance man—in her case, not a collector of premiums, but a nationally recognized expert in the field. William Avery Hyde had even written a book on the subject. After 1942 he raised his family in Columbus, Ohio, and sent three of his children, including Ruth, the youngest, to Antioch College in Yellow Springs.

Known, then as now, for a freewheeling political liberalism, the school met no more than half of Ruth's moral needs. By contrast, it was the mix of social awareness and spirtuality that drew her to the Society of Friends, which she joined in 1951. In the Quaker faith that would govern her life, those elements came together, each animated by a belief in the possibility of direct communication between the individual and the heavens. "That mystical aspect was very important to me."

She spent the years following her graduation in Quaker-ism's great American stronghold, southeastern Pennsylvania, teaching physical education to elementary schoolchildren at Germantown Friends and, before that, leading a "golden-age" group—"they'd practically all come over from Russia in '05"—at the Philadelphia YM-YWHA.

Seven years after Ruth's departure from the Y, Mr. Lewis Kohn, its business manager, would fondly recall this young woman who was placed only "with great reservation and hesita-tion" among the golden-agers, "inasmuch as these older per-sons were difficult to please, were obstinate and set in their ways." And yet, "it was not long before she had the members of her group in complete accord with her. They were teaching her Yiddish and were following her direction in every manner . . . when she left the employ of the YM-YWHA the members of her group were sad to see her leave."

Ruth Avery Hyde met Michael Ralph Paine at a folk dance in 1955, and they soon began attending Quaker Meeting together. "I liked the Quakers' church," Michael recalls today. In fact, he'd gone to Meeting even before becoming interested in Ruth. "The only reason I wasn't a Quaker was because they didn't sing. They didn't have music in their service." Fortunately, Ruth liked music, too; she and Michael would spend several years in mad-rigal singing-groups before and after their marriage, which took place in December of '57 at the Providence Monthly Meeting in Media, Pennsylvania.

Michael, four years older than his wife, had flunked out of Harvard in the late 1940s. A handsome dreamer, his head full of designs for mechanical devices and social betterment, he'd transferred to Swarthmore and spent a year there as a physics major, near the bottom of his class, before quitting college for good in June of 1951.

Michael's stepfather, Arthur Young, inventor of the world's first commercially licensed helicopter, the Bell 47, had a serious interest in both extrasensory perception and astrology, and both Paines can still recall the prospects of comfort and trouble he saw in their stars. Ruth remembers: "He looked at our charts once and said, 'You're really more like brother and sister.' And it made sense to me. I couldn't read the charts, but I feel *kindred* to Michael, that we are kin in some ways, whether it's equally good at denial, or repressing anger, or whatever it might be. Equally honest," she adds, accentuating the positive, "and wanting to live good lives." Michael more or less concurs in the fraternal diagnosis, though he'd characterize the condition as being "soulmates of a sort."

Both were questers, seekers of enlightenment, Ruth in a particular religious way she only hoped her husband could share. On August 15, 1956, before they were married, she composed on her typewriter a long prayer, part of it directly addressed to Michael:

When I cry now, I cry out of the overflow of the richness
of life.

And it is this, *this* that I seek. That I find essential . . . to my
   path, to my being, to all that I do.
And I must find out whether you know this overflow of life,
   this richness, and whether you want it.

She had little doubt that her future spouse also sought "to glorify
life, and make it much larger than the everyday," but she had to
face her anxiety that his way of accomplishing all this might not
be hers:

I think it's possible that I could be led from the things I
   most value, because of the lesser value I have of sharing
   deeply with a person I love.
And loving Michael, I would want to share what he finds
   most valuable, and look to beauty, and art, and music,
   and yet *miss* in it, that which takes *him* to *his* goal, and
   forget that which takes me to mine.
The same Goal. But a loss of my path, in an effort to travel
   to that goal on his path. And therefore, a loss of the goal,
   as well.

Dear God. Guide me. Oh, guide me.

Michael himself recognized, early on, a divergence between
these two shy souls, so apparently compatible that "people
thought we were married before we were, thought we were a
couple before we were." Sometimes "Ruth would get antsy, wig-
gling her foot just at the point in conversation when I started to
get interested." And there was the question of passion—whether

it would be sufficient and enduring. Michael remembers: "I had never loved Ruth very much. I've told her that. We met, and I told her that before we were married, and she said, 'Well, you go find someone you love.' And I was separated from her for a year, and then I came back, and hadn't found somebody I really loved, and I asked her again. I thought I needed to have a wife. And she thought I would grow to love her. And so we were married." When the Quaker elders came around for a prenuptial inspection, he was "terrified that they would ask me how I loved Ruth. They didn't. They looked in the closets to see if there was enough closet space. Yes, they find no problem!"

The couple set up house in a barn on the Youngs' property in Paoli, where Michael worked for his stepfather, making helicopter models and experimenting with aeronautical designs of his own. Arthur Young was able to pursue interests like astrology because of the extraordinary patent he had sold to Larry Bell in 1941. "That's his helicopter!"—the one hanging above the escalator in New York's Museum of Modern Art—Ruth confirms with delight, still admiring the way Young first established himself as a scientist and "*then* . . . got into the cosmic things that had interested him all his life."

In 1959, Michael Paine took a job with Bell Helicopter in Fort Worth, Texas. He and Ruth rented and soon purchased a house in nearby Irving, the fastest-growing city in the state. Founded in 1903 by Otis Brown and J. O. Schulze of the Rock Island Railroad survey team, Irving, according to one story, had been christened with the surname of Mrs. Brown's favorite American author. Through the Second World War, it remained a flat sort of sleepy hollow, a truck-farming pantry that supplied Dallas with its chickens and milk. (J. O. Schulze was still in Dallas County in 1959, when Ruth and Michael settled on West Fifth Street.) But between 1950 and 1960 Irving's population soared from 2,600 to nearly 46,000. It was the surrounding area's new manufacturing and electronics operations that brought a lot of the migrants, including the Paines.

But when the couple purchased their piece of the Western Hills Addition development, Michael and Ruth were not so much planting themselves on American-dream crabgrass as wandering deep into alien corn. "I was very lonely in Texas," says Ruth. "I felt isolated in terms of belief systems." Most Irvingites worshipped in churches like Kirkwood United Methodist, a few blocks up from the Paine house. Quakers were especially thin on the ground; the local Friends held their Meeting at a Seventh Day Adventist school by the Central Expressway in Dallas. Michael found his religious home in that city's First Unitarian congregation. His solidarity with Ruth—the soul mating he describes—helped the two of them to weather the unfamiliar mental climate that greeted them on the Texas prairie. "We were on the same side," he says.

For all that Texas represented an exotic departure, the Paines did not start off there entirely on their own. The couple always lived quite modestly—their Philadelphia accounts at Wanamaker's and Bonwit Teller never went above a high credit of $25, and they assumed a mortgage in Irving of under $10,000—but they had a thick financial cushion under them. Three years after Michael's maternal grandmother, Elise Cabot Forbes, died in 1960, his share of her legacy was worth a quarter of a million dollars.

The Paines' money was old by New England standards, let alone Texas ones. But neither Michael nor his wife had any real appetite for it. The inheritance that challenged and to some extent beset them was a cultural one, a highly refined pedigree that ran through both Michael's bloodlines. In their displaced way, he and Ruth represented a modern marriage of *Puritan Boston and Quaker Philadelphia,* the title of E. Digby Baltzell's noted study.

George Lyman Paine, Jr., Harvard '22, Michael's architect father, had involved himself with Trotskyite politics in 1930s New York; the young writer Dwight Macdonald helped manage the city-council race that Lyman Paine ran on the Socialist Workers ticket. By the time of his thirty-fifth college reunion, Lyman might have given up on Trotsky, but not, he wrote for the class report, on "a stubborn, active and uncompromising hostility to all forces, all aspects of society which deny to man both order and human dignity." During the fifties he edited a paper called *Correspondence,* "through which the ordinary worker can freely express his real concerns." He remained a security-index subject to the FBI.

Over time, his ex-wife and Michael's mother, Mrs. Arthur Young, would join the World Federalists, found the International Peace Academy, and, along with Arthur Young, establish the Institute for the Study of Consciousness in Berkeley. The Forbeses had combined substantial wealth and civic involvement for at least a century before Mrs. Young's childhood in Milton, Massachusetts. Her uncle, William Cameron Forbes, who never married but remained a life partner in the family's investment business, J. M. Forbes & Co., is characterized by the *Dictionary of American Biography* as "a willing public servant and a gentleman dilettante in the age of professional expertise." A star polo player, he was President Taft's governor-general in the Philippines and Herbert Hoover's ambassador to Japan.

His father, William Hathaway Forbes, had been the first president of the Bell Telephone Company, whose product had attracted early investment by *his* father, John Murray Forbes. As a young man in their counting house in Canton, J. M. Forbes vastly increased the family's money through the China trade, before coming home to finance the expansion of several railroads past the Mississippi and into the Midwest. Baltzell pronounces him "the most powerful Boston capitalist of his day." A strict abolitionist, he organized Negro regiments in Massachusetts and set up the Loyal Publication Society to propagandize for the Union cause. "Wherever he moved he was the benefactor," wrote Ralph Waldo Emerson, who delighted in seeing his daughter Edith marry Forbes's son.

Edith Emerson and William Hathaway Forbes became engaged on March 4, 1865, the day Lincoln gave his Second Inaugural address before a glowering John Wilkes Booth in the crowd at the Capitol. Nine days later, Emerson commended Edith to her fiancé's father, telling John Murray Forbes in a letter that "she does not please in advance as much as she merits, but can sometimes surprise old friends who tho't they knew her well, with deeper & better traits. She is humble, which is the basis of nobility."

One imagines the willowy, deeply well-intentioned Ruth

Paine, laughing gaily but often looking shyly at the ground, striking the latter-day Forbeses in much the same way when she married into Michael's family a hundred years later and began making summer visits to the Forbes compound on Naushon Island in Buzzard's Bay.

Michael has been in many ways more Forbes than Paine, but if one skips back several generations, over the architects and clergymen and poets on his paternal side, one reaches the considerable figure of Robert Treat Paine, a member of both Continental Congresses, who rode into Philadelphia with his colleagues on May 10, 1775. As Pauline Maier describes the scene in *American Scripture:*

> Some two hundred "principal Gentlemen, on Horseback, with their Swords Drawn," who met the delegations six miles outside the city, led the way into Philadelphia. Behind them came the city's new militia officers, two by two, also with swords drawn, then Hancock and Samuel Adams in an open four-wheeled carriage or phaeton (Hancock looking, one account suggested, somewhat sick), John Adams and Cushing in a two-wheeled "chaise," Robert Treat Paine, the New York and some Connecticut delegates—and, finally, a mass of additional participants in perhaps a hundred more horse-drawn carriages.

The end result of this colonial procession, fourteen months later, assured the peculiar fact that on the morning of November 22, 1963, Lee Harvey Oswald, preparing to go watch a modern political parade, would awaken in the bedroom, not only of Ralph Waldo Emerson's great-great grandson, but also the distant scion of a man who had signed the Declaration of Independence.

# Three

O n November 8, 1960, Ruth Paine passed up the chance to vote for a fellow Quaker in order to help elect, as the thirty-fifth President of the United States, a candidate pledged to stepping up missile production. Her pacifism had never been absolute, and she did not believe in unilateral disarmament. She was a Democrat, had cast her first presidential vote for Stevenson four years ago, and was delighted to be, this time, with what looked like a progressive-minded winner. The pleasure she took in John Kennedy's policies was "rather more, very likely, than [that of] Texans in general."

Four days before the election, a soon-legendary "Mink Coat Mob" of right-wing women, egged on by the city's Republican congressman, Bruce Alger, had jostled and spat upon Lyndon and Lady Bird Johnson, the vice-presidential candidate and his wife, as they entered the Adolphus Hotel for a rally. The local political atmosphere, already unbreathable to liberals, would grow distinctly toxic once Kennedy actually took office.

But on election night Ruth and Michael felt gay enough to host a little party mixing some of the old and new elements in their married life. Most of the guests were connected to Bell

Helicopter, but Ray and Ilse Entenmann, friends from Philadelphia days, came to the house, too. The Entenmanns were even more newly Texan than the Paines: Ray and Ilse, who'd moved down for his new job directing the Fort Worth Art Museum, had yet to meet the residency requirement for voting.

"We used to sing in the barn where the helicopter was invented," says Mr. Entenmann, still in Dallas today, as he recalls the beginning of his friendship with the Paines; Michael's mother had been one of Ray's students at the Pennsylvania Academy of Fine Arts. Her son and Ruth were, he says, on "absolutely the same wavelength as us in Philadelphia, and also for the short time that we knew them here. Intellectually we were very similar." Ilse Entenmann remembers that, on election night 1960 in Irving, she and her husband, aside from the Paines, "were the only Democrats in the house—and we kept quiet!"

Ruth and Michael had now been in Texas for a year, but "I don't think I ever adjusted," Michael says today. "We were in the midst of a lot of people uncomprehending of our way of living." Ruth remembers her own nostalgia for Pennsylvania: "My neighbors were very pleasant, and I enjoyed being with them, but it was not the kind of friendships that I'd had back in the east." She was tired, too. Her daughter Lynn had been born just after the move to Irving, and when the new parents "tried going to a concert, I'd fall asleep. Couldn't handle chamber music after 7 p.m.!" By the time of the election she was already six months pregnant with a second child, Christopher, who arrived on February 8, 1961.

Ruth's parents also preoccupied her, from a distance. After

more than thirty years of marriage, William Hyde had committed his wife to an Ohio sanitarium to be treated for paranoia and
delusions, an action Ruth had doubts about. Her position put
her in conflict with both her father and her brother, Carl, now a
doctor; but it did not free her from feelings of guilt. She wondered, in a letter to the sanitarium director, Dr. George T. Harding III, whether she might have contributed, accidentally, to
the conduct that led to her mother's confinement. The Hydes
finally divorced in 1961, and Ruth's mother, Carol, was soon
well enough to begin ministerial studies at Oberlin, with a view
toward becoming a hospital chaplain. In a letter to Ruth, Mrs.
Hyde confessed to feeling under a "terrific and constant strain"
to prove her competence to her ex-husband and other two children—though "not you, thank God!"

It's little wonder that, during this period, Ruth found herself
more happily stimulated by Michael's family than her own. "I
just liked *all* the people in [his] family," Paines and Forbeses,
she says. Socially, "they all sensed an obligation to do something." Lyman Paine still "wanted to save the world and wanted
to know, 'Well, what are *you* doing to save the world?' " Lyman's
second wife, Freddy—if less nobly obliged than Ruth's actual
mother-in-law, Mrs. Young—seemed nonetheless rather awesome: "A remarkable lady," Ruth recalls, someone who'd once
done labor-organizing in the coal mines, "riding the rails from
town to town and then getting out her skirt when she got there."

All these models proved less comfortably inspirational to
Michael himself. Growing up after his parents' divorce, he
hadn't seen much of Lyman but was lastingly impressed by the

few political meetings to which his father had brought him. Even today he can recall "the idealism, the zeal, the dedication of all the people that I met there." Yet he also remembers feeling himself to be "a drag, an impediment to [Lyman's] functioning in the things he wanted to do."

The Forbes legacy was similarly daunting. On Naushon Island, "around the walls of the dining room . . . are forebears, engravings. And my grandfather's generation—Uncle Cam was one of the brothers—were remarkable people, and I totally gave up on trying to equal them . . . I didn't feel myself a direct example of them. But they set the picture for me—what one does, or should look for, what one should strive for in life. Chip off the old block in a certain sense, even though I don't feel I register on the chart."

Michael's own schemes for social improvement remained mental and abortive. A friend of Ruth, Carolyn Ruckdeschel, would tell the FBI that he "appeared to be a very brilliant individual, but seemed very immature and not ready to settle down . . . Michael had dreams of owning and operating his own factory, utilizing his own designs, and running everything according to his own whim." Even Ruth felt a certain discomfort in living up to Michael's family. At the end of 1959, a year before Michael received his grandmother's legacy, Mrs. Young presented the couple with a check for $1,500, which Ruth was reluctant to take, fearing it would obligate her to have a more beautifully decorated home than she was capable of achieving.

The Quaker writer Jessamyn West, who would briefly enter the Paines' lives in the mid-1960s, published a little book called

*Love Is Not What You Think* during the year they moved to Texas. Michael would come to regard it as the best thing he'd read on the subject, partly perhaps because of its assertion that a woman

> cannot, herself loving and desirous, be partnered by a man who does not love her, yet takes her. There is a reversal of the male and female roles here which damages not only her image of herself, but, even more important, her image of the man.

The strain of trying to do the right thing—in the world and toward each other—imperiled Ruth and Michael's marriage from the start. As he took pains to be honest about his lack of feeling, she forced herself to be brave; both scarred themselves with candor and civility. By July 1961, the Paines already had separate checking accounts; by the following spring, tired of emotional ambiguities, Ruth asked Michael to state his reasons for remaining in the marriage. When he answered it "was easier and cost less" to stay, she requested that he move out by the time she got back from her usual round of summer travels. By September of '62, Michael had relocated to an apartment in Arlington.

Friends and family thought the separation a shame, but if they felt inclined to blame anyone, it was Michael, for what some called introversion, others self-centeredness. As it was, the Paines' moviegoing and madrigal singing continued, and whenever Michael was about to visit Ruth and the children in the Irving house, her heart and step would lighten. Nonetheless, Michael recalls, it would eventually be Ruth "who wanted to divorce, and [was] courageous . . . I was prepared to stay in my traces in Texas, and she was the one who urged, wanted divorce." Honesty demanded as much. "But I still liked her," says Michael. "I had no quarrel with her."


Ruth had been studying Russian since 1957—at Berlitz, on phonograph records, in summer classes at Penn and Middlebury. Her interest in the language itself was only increased by participation in the Young Friends organization, specifically its East—West Contacts Committee, which sponsored the American travels of three young Soviets—a journalist, a factory worker, and an economics student—in 1958. Ruth helped with preparations for their tour and met the Russians at a party in Philadelphia, but she was not one of the five Americans who accompanied them throughout the U.S. She had more direct involvement with the Young Friends' pen-pal program, a good-will exchange set up with the Committee of Soviet Youth Organizations. Nina Aparina, of Krasnodar, became Ruth's correspondent and eventually the astounded recipient of a Christmas photo taken in an obviously balmy Texas.

Ruth's intensive Russian study at Middlebury, in the summer of '59, came just before the move to Irving and Lynn's birth. It was an overreach: She had pried a last-minute opening out of a director who "was right to turn me down the first time," since her language skills simply weren't strong enough for the program's immersion technique. She promised "to speak the entire summer nothing but Russian," and the experience proved "kind of lonely," a rarefied preview of what awaited her in Texas.

But it also represented "a last chance to do something away from home," a motivation her husband credited more easily than others did. As she wrote her mother, who was skeptical of her plans:

> I feel Michael's support for my going—and feel that going will not injure what we have in our marriage that we want to keep.—Support from the culture, so to speak, is as you would expect—negative.—Expressed by acquaintances by [an] "Is Michael going too?" or "How does Michael feel about that?" or "I wouldn't feel right being away from my husband that long."

Four years later, in the winter of 1963, the Rev. Carol Hyde, newly accustomed to independence from her own husband, would be delighted that her daughter was now proficient enough in Russian to have lined up a summer job tutoring the language at Dallas's St. Mark's School. "Great!" she wrote Ruth on February 12. "Let's hope enough students sign up."

That same February, Everett Glover, with whom she'd sung madrigals here, recalled her linguistic interest when he started planning a get-together at his home in Highland Park. One of his guests would be a young American who'd spent time in the USSR. The chance for Ruth to converse in Russian with the fellow's Soviet wife might be a treat for both women.

*"Everett's?"* The notation, still visible in the square labeled "Washington's Birthday" on Ruth's 1963 Hallmark pocket calendar, was not meant, by its question mark, to indicate any lack of enthusiasm for attending Glover's party—not even after

Michael came down with a bad cold and decided not to join Ruth there. It reflected only Glover's save-the-date tentativeness in the first of two phone calls he made with the invitation. Even so, it's hard not to see, in the little interrogative, a life poised over its own fate, still able to tip one way and avoid it, or plunge straight down to what it held.

February 22nd fell on a Friday, one day after President Kennedy sent Congress his proposal for Medicare, the sort of social-betterment program that kept Ruth one of his enthusiastic supporters. Another item in the same day's news—the feckless attack by two Cuban aircraft against a drifting American shrimp boat—was the sort of story more likely to interest the guest holding forth in Everett Glover's kitchen when Ruth Paine first laid eyes upon him. With his soft voice and receding hairline, twenty-three-year-old Lee Oswald appeared much less exotic than his experience, which he now eagerly recounted to a small group of partygoers. They asked him, Ruth remembers, "why he went to the Soviet Union, and what his impressions were." Everett had not told her that the young man had actually been a defector, but Oswald, currently employed in the photo department of a graphic-arts company, now spoke critically of the USSR, where he'd begged to stay in the fall of '59, just as Ruth was beginning to accommodate herself to Texas.

"He really enjoyed being the center of attention," says Ruth, but that night she paid him less of it than did the other listeners. She was eager to meet Oswald's wife, busy at that point in the bedroom, taking care of the couple's baby girl. "I wanted to see if I could talk with her, if we could communicate." In the event, they managed to, though Ruth felt too embarrassed by her own Russian to say much.

She was taken by something in this girl, a full decade younger than herself and so obviously isolated. Here was the chance—in future, less hectic circumstances—to speak Russian with someone; and here, too, was an opportunity, yet perceived only dimly, for Ruth to alleviate her own loneliness. Both possibilities played a part in her asking for Marina Oswald's address. Ruth drove home with it that night, out of Dallas, below Love Field, and back into Irving. Her relationship with the Oswalds had begun its exact nine-month gestation toward another Friday.

# Four

Twenty-four hours after Everett Glover's party, Marina Oswald tried to kill herself.

That February Lee had been regularly beating his wife, and on Saturday the 23rd, in the worst fit of temper he'd ever thrown—over the way she'd prepared his supper—he started to choke her. A fortuitous cry from Junie made him desist, but later the same evening he found Marina standing atop the toilet, attempting to hang herself with a length of clothesline. Oswald halted the strangulation that, a little while earlier, he had tried to accomplish himself.

Ruth did not know that most of Dallas's small community of

Russian emigres had already washed their hands of the couple. They might still see Marina as one of them, but they'd decided Lee was a grandiose lout. Some of the Russians had noticed the bruises; if his wife kept going back to him it was, finally, her problem. One woman from the group who had been helpful the previous fall, not many months after the Oswalds' arrival from the USSR, regarded his defection to that country as *prima facie* evidence of mental problems, and none of his more recent behavior had changed her mind.

Within a week of meeting Marina, Ruth made use of the address she'd asked for and sent a note to 214 Neely Street. (The Oswalds had no phone.) In reply, Marina thanked her twice for "not forgetting us"—as so many people who spent time around the couple preferred to do. During March, the two women visited, twice in Dallas and then in Irving, and introduced their small children to one another. "You don't know how much I enjoyed being at your home and in your company," Marina wrote afterwards. "I say this sincerely, without flattery. And not only because I don't get to go anywhere, but also because I feel at ease with you, as at home." She also felt safe there.

A supper in Irving, at which Michael and Lee could get acquainted, was arranged for Tuesday, April 2. "I regretted that I hadn't had a chance to meet this fellow," Michael remembers, pretty sure Ruth organized the dinner to make up for that. He drove into Dallas to pick up the carless Oswalds and in the event didn't much like his first impression of Lee: "He was speaking to [Marina] in Russian, scolding her, I think, for being slow to be packed up [with the baby's things] . . . And I think I told him that Ruth was not one to get too upset about being a little bit late.

I didn't tell him [exactly] that, but I did tell him this isn't a great matter. But his tone of voice toward Marina, and her having to take these whiplashes meekly and quietly and obediently, was offensive to me." Over the next seven months, where Oswald was concerned, nothing would bother Michael more than Lee's refusal to let Marina learn English.

Oswald remained curt to Marina through dinner. Ruth was already allowing her dislike of him to form, even if it went against her nature to let such an attitude harden. "I think," she says, "he was pretty satisfied with his view of how life was, in the sense that he had it figured out." Which is to say that his kind were ripe for exploitation, and that he didn't get enough credit for what he did—or was capable of. Michael remembers him complaining about how his boss at the photo shop got paid enough to own a Chrysler. The subject of Edwin A. Walker, the rabble-rousing right-wing general, also came up briefly. "It would have been hard to avoid talking about Walker at the time," Michael now points out—the general was both a local and national celebrity—and a "peculiar smile" crossed Oswald's face at the mention of Walker's name. But Michael didn't pursue the topic very far. "I was wanting to get along with this fellow."

Ruth knew the Oswalds were expecting a second child, and over supper she held her tongue about a distressing piece of information that Marina had imparted during one of their March visits: Lee wanted to send his wife back to Russia. Already trying to figure out how she might help avert this, Ruth sat down on Sunday, April 7, to draft a letter she didn't intend to mail, but whose composition would help her to find the Russian words for an offer she might soon deliver in person:

I want to invite you to move here and live with me both now and later when the baby is born. I don't know how things are for you at home with your husband, I don't know what would be better for you, June and Lee,—to live together or apart. It is, of course, your affair, and you have to decide what is better and what you wish to do. But I want to say that you have a choice. When you wish, for days, weeks, months, you could move here. I want you to consider "2515 W. 5th Street" your second home. I have already thought about this invitation a lot. It is not a quick thought.

In exchange for Marina's help with Russian, Ruth would pay for all the groceries and incidentals; Lee could cover medical expenses and clothes. Marina could sleep with June in the front bedroom, and perhaps help a little with the housekeeping—not Ruth's strong suit. "In the course of two weeks you could learn all I know about cooking."

The idea was bold—she had seen this girl only a handful of times—and somewhat dangerous, too. She remembers feeling that, if she made the offer and Marina accepted it, she would be "taking on some of the role of support that [Lee] would feel was his, and I wanted to be sure he didn't feel undercut or supplanted in any way by my actions." In a later portion of her unsent letter, she put the matter gently, encouraging Marina to regard the two of them as being in a similar situation: "I don't want to hurt Lee. Of course I don't know what he wants. Perhaps he feels like Michael, who at one time wants and doesn't want to live with me."

Ruth's religion and character told her to seek and spread light, but from this point on, for the nearly eight months that follow, the two adults who dominate her emotional life, Michael and Marina, will be keeping her in the dark.

According to Ruth's datebook, she and Marina may have visited on April 11. Then or later, Marina did not disclose that the man responsible for that week's big news story—an attempt to kill General Walker—was her husband. She had known it since the night of April 10 when Lee departed on his mission and she found his list of written instructions about what she should do if he was captured. Despite her recent suicide attempt, Marina had a strong instinct for survival. She said nothing to Ruth, and she held on to the incriminating list, knowing it might one day provide useful leverage against her "crazy husband," Lee.

Michael Paine, from the first hour he met him, had known something equally crucial about Oswald. But his information, too, would be kept from Ruth, for thirty years.


By the middle of April, Lee had lost his job at the graphic-arts company and decided to seek work in New Orleans, his birthplace, where he still had family. Ruth learned this on Wednesday, April 24, when she arrived at Neely Street for a planned visit with Marina and found Lee headed for the bus station. He had a cumbersome load of suitcases and duffel bags, so she offered to drive him to the terminal, several blocks from Dealey Plaza. His plan was to have Marina join him in Louisiana once he found a job.

Ruth now took the chance to suggest that Marina and Junie stay with her in Irving until Lee was ready to call for them—an arrangement that suddenly suited everyone's convenience and pride. Lee had a more compelling reason to get out of town than he did to protest Ruth's kindness: The police were still looking for Walker's would-be assassin.

Soon after Marina moved into the front bedroom on West Fifth, Ruth wrote her own mother about what good company the younger woman was, even if Ruth's still-imperfect Russian made communication laborious. In fact, both women experienced some of the linguistic isolation Ruth had once felt at Middlebury; the household's other voices, two-year-old Chris and $3\frac{1}{2}$-year-old Lynn, were learning the Russian nouns for items like "diaper" before picking up their English equivalents.

The mothers worked hard, dealing with pinworms and children's quarrels: "One day Chris and June were squabbling over a toy and I commented: 'Soviet–American cultural exchange.' [Marina] laughed and said: 'Don't say it.' " For all its drudgery, this brief period, little more than two weeks, would stand out as a kind of feminine idyll, a respite from male boorishness and inattention. It came to an abrupt close on May 9 with a phone call from Lee. He had found work—a job he would loathe, greasing coffee machines—and he wanted his wife to come to New Orleans.

"*Papa nas lubet!*"—"Papa loves us!"—Marina exclaimed to Junie. Ruth's love was easily come by; a return of Lee's made for victory and resurgent pride. "I don't know what drew them to each other," Ruth says, but she could "see there was a bonding" between husband and wife, and she took pains not to throw cold water on Marina's enthusiasm. She did not know the couple's shared secret of Oswald's violence—against General Walker and Marina herself; and so, one day after Lee's phone call, doing what she felt was right, Ruth drove Marina to New Orleans.

Lee appeared proud of the apartment he'd found on Magazine Street. Ruth and her two children spent three nights there, and while the trip created a few pleasant memories—some sightseeing at Lake Ponchartrain—Ruth was soon unsettled by the cockroaches and the bickering. She and the children slept on pallets and "kind of made a ring of bug spray" around themselves. Marina, having had a spell of modern suburban comforts back in Irving, seemed less impressed than Lee by this apartment and began picking at her husband over things like his attempt to make wine from blackberries. Whatever blows she'd taken from him, Marina was not wholly without defensive weaponry: "She certainly did get irritated and speak back very sharply to him," Ruth recalls. "And of course, having better facility in Russian, she usually got the better of a verbal argument."

For all their volatility and poor financial prospects, Ruth did think the Oswalds might take root in New Orleans, and soon after getting home to Texas, she was wistful for Marina's company. There was no longer anyone with whom to share the bottle boiling and the laundry folding; and, rather disappointingly, her Russian class at St. Mark's ended up consisting of a single tutee, Bill Hootkins, whose father paid Ruth directly. Within days of getting home, Ruth found in Michael's desk her typewritten 1956 "Prayer" ("I want to be free,—in my marriage, in

my life, to pursue this path of increased belief") and removed it
to her iron file box, as if her feelings could no longer belong to
anyone but herself.

Her first letter to Marina in New Orleans describes matters
as humorously as possible:

> Home again, and everything as usual: the floor must be
> washed, and dishes, clothes. Especially dull after our visit
> which was interesting and unusual . . . Michael didn't call to
> ask about my trip and finally I called him at work since he
> never was at home in his apartment. Today I'm angry with
> him and intend to go to New York to look for a lover! He
> loves his machines—and that's all!

Marina's emotional fortunes had taken an even more sudden
downturn. She replies to Ruth on May 25: "As soon as you left all
'love' stopped, and I am very hurt that Lee's attitude toward me
is such that I feel each minute that I bind him." She recognizes a
fundamental unhappiness linking her to Ruth: "Lee has said to
me that he doesn't love me,—so you see we came to mistaken
conclusions. It is hard for you and me to live without a return of
our love,—interesting, how will it all end?"

There was supposed to be a practical aspect to the correspondence: Marina would correct the Russian in Ruth's letters and
send them back to Texas. But the emotional interchange out-
weighed the linguistic one. "Everything you do and think is interesting to me," Ruth tells Marina on June 1, in the same letter
containing the news that she's made an appointment (later can-
celled) with a divorce lawyer. Marina, whom Oswald was trying

to keep from seeing any Russians in New Orleans, tries to console Ruth, not only with the truth that misery loves company—"you are not the only rejected one in this world"—but also with a sort of forlorn optimism: "Surely a person can carry on through all the most heavy losses, trials and misfortunes. I think we will not perish, but that something will smile brightly on us too. Don't you think so?"

Ruth had already begun inquiring about whether Marina might like to return to Texas for the baby's birth, expected in October, though she was careful to address the details about fees at Grand Prairie's Plattner Clinic to Lee directly. Her desire to bring Marina back became pressing in the second week of July, during a busy period that included separate visits from her parents, Ruth reread Marina's correspondence and noticed something she had earlier missed: mention of Lee's renewed insistence that his wife go back to the Soviet Union.

Alarmed, Ruth asked some Quaker and Unitarian connections in New Orleans to check on Mrs. Oswald, and, with Michael, she drew up definite financial arrangements under which Marina might come to Irving. In a letter written July 11, she gives Lee, as always, a wide berth:

I don't know how Lee feels, I would like to know. Surely things are hard for him now, too. I hope that he would be glad to see you with me where he can know that you and the children will receive everything that is necessary, and he would not need to worry about it. Thus he could start life again.

The following day she writes again, to suggest that Marina can't be made to go back to Russia without wanting to, but mostly to say: "I love you Marina, and want to live with you."

To the suggestion that she and Marina had a lesbian attachment, Ruth today replies, with a laugh, "No, that hadn't occurred to me!" She acknowledges that, even in '63, she remained "*very* lonely in Texas," and that her own vulnerability helped push her into aiding this foreign girl; but what she still hears, in the apparently romantic tone of her letters, is an attempt to reassure the younger woman, who "doubted her acceptability" and her own worthiness of Ruth's assistance: "I was trying to say, 'We can be friends here.' " As for Oswald's own possible homosexuality—a matter still interesting to students of his months in New Orleans—she never had a thought in that direction. But "you have to understand how naive I was. Would I have known?" Marina talked only of the girlfriends Lee had had prior to meeting her.

Marina herself was afraid to discuss the Texas invitation with Lee. She tried instead to assure Ruth that things were better between them ("for a considerable period he has been good to me"), but Ruth's extended hand did draw from the young Soviet woman a flood of pro-American sentiment: "I love your people and your country and I thank you, and all, that you are such good people. God grant there would always be peace-time, and that people would treat each other only so." She promised to keep Ruth's offer as an ace in the hole, should Lee again treat her badly: "Sweet Ruth, I am so thankful to you for your good and sympathetic heart."

———

From her days in the co-op program at Antioch College, which required her to drive from one far-flung job to another, Ruth had been a confident traveler. Late summer 1963 found her tracing a great zigzag from Texas to New England to the Midwest to the deep South. Her two small children would see a lot of the U.S.A in their mother's '55 Chevrolet, but the trio's odyssey did not take in the era's usual high points of automotive sightseeing. Ruth's Hallmark datebook for August and September, suddenly unfestooned with dental appointments and school-board voting reminders, looks as blank as the open road, but she was in fact following a complex itinerary designed to connect her with an array of family members and old friends, as well as new, self-imposed obligations.

She made it from Irving to Massachusetts in about five days and spent the early part of August at the Forbes property on Naushon Island. She later saw the Youngs in Paoli, her mother in Columbus, and her brother in Yellow Springs. All along the way she visited Quakers she'd known since the fifties, when they were all involved with the Young Friends: Mary Forman in Hartford; David Houghton and his wife Barbara in Washington, D.C.; the families of Wilmer Stratton and Paul Lacey in Richmond, Indiana, where both men taught at Earlham College, a Quaker school. Almost all her hosts would later recall her talking—more comfortably than she could of Michael—about the young Russian woman she was getting to know.

Late in August Marina sent a letter to Paoli, mentioning that

Lee was once again out of work but hoping "that everything will clear up, right?" She did not mention that he was spending some of his idle time on the Magazine Street porch dry-firing the same rifle he had used against General Walker. She looked forward to a visit from Ruth that was set for the third week of September.

Remembering her long journey now, Ruth cheerfully brushes off any estimation of the efficiency and stamina it must have required. All the travel was just "part of how I solved the loneliness and distance from family." If there was one thing she failed to accomplish this time, it was the side trip to the Washington Mall to hear Dr. King, which she could have made while seeing the Houghtons and her sister. The missed opportunity nagged at her a little, and more so after news came on Sunday, September 15, while she was visiting the Laceys and Strattons in Richmond, Indiana, that four young girls had been killed in the bombing of Birmingham's Sixteenth Street Baptist Church.

It had been here in Richmond, one night years ago, on a visit to Earlham College, that young Ruth Hyde had felt herself overwhelmed with religious feeling. She recorded the experience, with cross-outs and misspellings, on lined notebook paper:

> I steered Nancy off the wall leading to Earlham Hall and led
> her to a large tree where we sat down. Here I thought I might
> be able to get in touch with God. I cryed silently for some
> time. The stars above blinked down on me. People contin-
> ued to come out of Carpenter Hall—But I didn't notice them.

Now back near the site of this long-ago illumination, Ruth decided, the morning after the church bombing, that she would travel to New Orleans via Birmingham. "I thought," she recalls thirty-seven years later—a month after one of the bombers was finally convicted—"well, I can stop there. It's not a crowd, you know. I'll just stop and pay my respects, make a donation, and if there are folks who [are there], stand with them. I felt I could explain it to my kids, sort of."

After this short pilgrimage—to the second most memorable act of violence in 1963—she arrived in New Orleans on Friday, September 20, expecting just to visit. Despite her husband's unemployment, Marina Oswald seemed cheerful and wanted Ruth to have a good time. She proposed a tour of Bourbon Street, without Lee. "It was so obvious that we were out of place," Ruth recollects with a smile. "A pregnant mother and her baby, and a mother and her two small toddlers, peering into the doorways. And the people peered back with a good-grief-what-are-you-doing-here look on their faces. So we didn't stay very long."

The little outing recalled last May's household in Irving—an arrangement that was about to reconstitute itself. Far from feeling threatened, Lee now "seemed relieved . . . to have [Marina] come back with me, and to know that I could translate to get her into the hospital, things like that." He let Ruth believe he was going to look for work in Houston or maybe even Philadelphia, a city she'd spoken of. But Marina knew the truth: Once she and Ruth were gone, Lee would be heading for Mexico City in search of a visa to Cuba. She said nothing to her friend.

Ruth remembers Lee being unusually helpful on Monday morning, the 23rd, when it came time to load up the station wagon. The back of it was soon full of Marina's belongings and his own, which it was understood he would come for at some point. Only after the car was packed did he and the departing travelers notice a soft tire. "So we had to unpack some and get to a gas station to buy a spare," Ruth recalls. The new purchase further obscured some of the vehicle's contents: "Instead of putting the spare tire *under* everything in the car, we put it on top, because that was an issue if we had a flat. We'd have to get everything out."

But nothing went wrong. Oswald bid a genuinely sad goodbye to his *devochki* (girls), and the car departed. Marina let out a cheer when she crossed the border into Texas, telling Ruth, somewhat surprisingly, that she thought of the state as her home. After a night in a motel, the women continued on to Irving, where Michael Paine was on hand to help unload the car.

Among the goods carried into the garage was a well-tied green-and-brown blanket roll containing a bolt-action Mannlicher-Carcano rifle. The only adult there who didn't know that Oswald owned it was Ruth—the only person who wouldn't have allowed it anywhere in the house.

# Five

On Friday, October 4, Ruth Paine donated blood at Parkland Hospital, where Marina soon would be delivering her baby at reduced cost. Later in the day, when Lee Oswald surprised his wife with a phone call announcing that he was at the bus station in Irving and would like Ruth to come pick him up, Marina said Ruth was still too weak to drive.

Oswald's call ended another two-week spell, like last May's, of near-constant companionship between Marina and Ruth. The absent father-to-be would continue to maintain that he'd spent the time hunting for work, unsuccessfully, in Houston. Upon showing up in Irving, he certainly did look defeated, though he had actually come from Mexico City, where he'd failed to get his visa for Cuba.

Now prepared to look for work in Dallas, he'd already gotten himself a bed at the Y, and would soon rent a $7-a-week room in the Oak Cliff neighborhood, near downtown. He could visit Marina on the weekends, if that was all right with Ruth. Once he was on his feet, perhaps after Christmas, he would get an apartment able to hold himself, his wife, and what would then be two children.

Ruth supplied Lee with a Dallas street map, whose job-hunting Xs would soon appear overly meaningful to those studying his possessions. His search for work was hampered, not just by lack of a car, but by his inability to drive. Ruth soon made plans to get him a learner's permit and give him lessons in the '55 Chevy.

Lee did seem to be making an effort. Ruth never expressed herself more positively about Oswald than she does in a letter written to her mother on October 14. During the two previous weekends, she says, he has proved himself "a happy addition to our expanded family. He played with Chris, watched football on TV, planed (filed?) down the doors that wouldn't close, and generally added a needed masculine flavor. From a poor first impression I have come to like him." Ruth's improved feelings were mostly a matter of hope and effort. One senses her, during this crucial week, trying to wish Oswald into something he could never be. On Saturday she writes her father that Lee has shown himself to be a "fine family man after all."

He has earned the title by taking a job. "Minimum wage & nothing special about it," Ruth reports to her mother, but she's pleased to see him happy. Characteristically, she takes no credit for having provided the successful lead. But on the morning of Monday, the 14th, after she and Marina had coffee down the street and Mrs. Linnie Mae Randle mentioned that they were still hiring at the warehouse where her brother worked, it was Ruth who had made the call to Mr. Roy Truly, manager of the Texas School Book Depository, to get Lee an interview. Upon showing up for it, he scored points with his potential new boss by calling him "Sir." On Friday night, when Lee came out to Irving after his third day at work, Ruth had a cake ready for his 24th birthday.

For the past two weeks she had been seeing to the needs of five people, not counting herself, and trying to engage in as much long-term thinking as the busy situation would admit. She seems even to have considered putting a trailer in the back-yard, should the house still be so full during her mother's planned February visit.

The house became more tightly packed with the birth of the Oswalds' second daughter on Sunday, the 20th. Ruth was at the hospital when the little girl arrived; the "fine family man," afraid Parkland would present him with a bill, stayed in Irving. Even today, Ruth doesn't blame him for this; he may have had a job, but he hardly had the money, and with the hospital's fast-discharge procedure for new mothers, Marina would be home in forty-eight hours. The baby was named Audrey Marina Rachel, the first name for Audrey Hepburn, star of *War and Peace*, which Marina and Ruth had seen together last May; Rachel was for a niece of Ruth's, and it was this third name that would stick, even though Lee didn't like its "Jewish" sound. The delivery proved trouble free; Ruth's blood, not required for it, may still have been on hand five Sundays later, when Rachel's father would bleed to death in the same hospital.

As they went about their weekday tasks, Ruth continued to recognize a "wall" in her companion, who guarded a sizeable precinct of privacy behind it. But the women were too busy with the babies to be much bothered by conversational gaps, which Marina sometimes filled with talk of plays and movies, retelling the plots of ones she'd seen years before in Minsk and Leningrad. This love of entertainment left her vulnerable to Lee's frequent charge that she was "bourgeois." So did her appreciation of Ruth's appliances, devices that did not feature prominently in the Russian book of housekeeping advice Lee had gotten his wife for her birthday the previous year, and which had found its way, through all the intervening moves, to West Fifth Street. "We liked comfort!" Ruth remembers, laughing at the memory of Oswald's scorn. "If that's bourgeois"—having a washing machine that works—"count me in."

Along with the inscrutable emotional support he could sometimes manage to offer Marina, the young Marxist could also object to the way she cooked his potatoes and ironed his shirts. "Picky, picky," says Ruth, who still remembers hearing the complaints, even if they couldn't be made so violently in Irving as they'd been on Neely Street back in February. On the weekdays, when Lee wasn't around, Marina would confide to Ruth some of her marriage's difficulties, including its sexual disappointments. Ruth suggested a visit to Planned Parenthood, which offered, in addition to birth-control information, counseling about "satisfaction."

Lee didn't lack all bourgeois tastes himself. On weekend nights he'd watch his war movies on the TV, and after he'd managed to secure a job he could get to by bus, he still let Ruth give him driving lessons. Time in the car was a rare occasion for them to be alone together. "I don't think he liked [Ruth] very much," says Michael Paine today. "He didn't expect people to be nice." Ruth herself says she continued to take pains to make him understand that she profited from Marina's presence in the house, "so that he wouldn't see it as a gift." But even gifts from God were suspicious to Oswald, who didn't like the Quaker grace Ruth said at weekend meals.

God, if He existed, was probably working an angle like everybody else. Michael remembers Oswald saying, about the newspaper, that "You can read between the lines and see what they want you to do." Both the Paines always found themselves more struck by Lee's lack of logic than any other mental failure, but his comment about the paper made Michael think he

must be very alone. He had previously spoken about the people he worked with at the photo company. He'd only described how they would talk about sports and you couldn't talk with them . . . He never did speak of anybody or any group being on the same side as he was. It was always a lone person fending off different kinds of angry, oppositional groups to him.

Michael claims never to have glimpsed in Oswald's expression the kind of fanaticism and "craziness" he saw in the eyes of local Birchers, when he dropped in on some right-wing gatherings out of curiosity and his own vague desire "to produce a rapprochement" in the political climate. He similarly came up with a reformer's idea for relieving Lee's political solitude: "I thought," Michael remembers, "Why don't I take him to the ACLU?" There Lee might meet some sympathetic people who could draw him out of his angry isolation. But when the two men attended a meeting of the group in Dallas on Friday night, October 25, Oswald expressed a baffled contempt that the organization existed to defend extant civil liberties rather than pursue its own program of political action. He didn't, in any case, have the emotional wherewithal to connect with any potential friends. "The world was kind of cardboard for him," Michael now realizes; a two-dimensional place, easily torn.

Just as Marina enjoyed using the Paines' washer, Lee, on his weekends in Irving, liked taking advantage of mechanical devices not available at his rooming house. At one point he employed the drill press Michael had in the garage to turn a souvenir peso he'd brought back from Mexico into something Marina could wear on a necklace. And on Saturday, November 9th, he sat down at Ruth's typewriter.

If Everett Glover's party and Ruth's coffee with Mrs. Randle (the book-depository job tip) are small events that might have constructed large alternate realities by not having happened at all, Oswald's work at Ruth's keyboard is one preliminary event that might have changed everything by happening just a bit differently. "I'd walked by while he was working at the typewriter," Ruth now remembers, "and he kind of leaned over as if he didn't want me to see" what he was composing. That didn't bother her; but the following morning, Sunday, she noted that he'd left out, in plain sight on her secretary desk, the handwritten draft he'd attempted to conceal while typing.

It was this apparent contradiction that caught Ruth's attention and made her feel, for the first time, that Oswald might not be "very well glued together." This, as well as an accidental glimpse of the letter's contents, compelled her to read the whole draft. In it, Oswald sought to inform the Soviet embassy in Washington of his unsuccessful visit to Mexico City, as well as the state of his relations with "the notorious FBI":

> The FBI is not now interested in my activities in the progressive organization FPCC [Fair Play for Cuba Committee] of which I was secretary in New Orleans, Louisiana, since I no longer live in that state.
>
> The FBI has visited us here in Texas. On Nov. 1st agent of the FBI James P. Hosty warned me that if I attempt to engage in FPCC activities in Texas the FBI will again take an "interest" in me.

The letter's subject matter magnified Ruth's distress: "The lies weren't large, but they were, you know, references that really disturbed me." Not knowing he'd been to Mexico City, she *thought* that was a lie. She knew more certainly, despite what he was now telling the Soviets, that the FBI did remain "interested" in him.

She also knew that Oswald had never met Agent Hosty. When the FBI man drove out on November 1 and November 5, only Ruth and Marina had been at home. His promise not to visit Oswald at the Book Depository reassured Ruth's sense of fairness. She later told Lee himself that, while he "could expect that [the FBI] would want to know where he was," he had no reason to worry. "I was trying to say . . . this is a country where you can have opinions that differ from the government viewpoint, and it's okay." Today, Hosty remembers Ruth as "well-educated, soft-spoken, and compassionate."

But the embassy letter, which she only found five days after Hosty's second visit, agitated Ruth as nothing about Oswald had previously. She would later tell investigators that his use of her typewriter to produce it had seemed particularly offensive. Norman Mailer, in his book *Oswald's Tale* (1995), sees Ruth's "buried sense of property" cropping out here. But he fails to understand the sort of ownership she would have felt Oswald was violating. This manual typewriter had followed her around since college, and its elite-size keys had hammered out her most painful and personal reflections, including the 1956 "Prayer" and her highly self-analytical letters to the director of the sanitarium where her mother was committed in 1960. The machine was more an instrument of intimacy than formality: the soul-searchings it had helped her conduct now sat boxed in that metal file, where there was even a school paper on "Capitalism" that Ruth Hyde had written at sixteen. By using the typewriter,

Oswald was intruding, not on her material goods, but on her lifetime of truth seeking.

Ruth was enough bothered by the embassy letter to make a fast, handwritten copy of it early Sunday morning, while Lee showered. This sort of surreptitiousness was out of character for Ruth, but the letter distressed her enough to make her think she might need to discuss it with Michael, or Agent Hosty, or Lee himself. It was one thing to welcome a past defector into your home; it was another to keep him there while he continued to make grandiose communication with Soviet officials. When she'd finished copying, she put Lee's rough draft back on top of the desk. The rest of the day was busy but tranquil. Michael visited; Ruth gave Lee another driving lesson; the TV broadcast another football game. Television might also have provided the treat of seeing Ruth's father, William Hyde, except that the Nationwide Insurance commercials he was then doing for Sunday's *Issues and Answers* program did not run in Texas: The company, whose symbol was a blanket, denoting the comfort and comprehensiveness of its coverage, didn't do business in the state.

Late Sunday afternoon, with still "enough strong men around," Ruth got Lee and Michael to help rearrange the living room furniture. She put Lee's draft of the embassy letter inside the secretary while it was repositioned. When the shift had been accomplished, she placed it back on the desktop. Lee never took the opportunity to say anything about it.

Ruth, however, could not get the letter off her mind. That night, while Oswald stayed up late watching television, she sat down beside him. Their moments alone might be infrequent and uncomfortable, but this one proved the occasion for his sympathetic remark about her impending divorce, and she wanted to stretch the unusual mood into a chance for him to explain the letter. But she could not bring herself to. "You know," she says today, "I was skirting the edge of trying to be sure that he didn't see me as an enemy, and I think that would have made him feel as if I was attacking. So I wasn't about to do that." As Bill Hyde's daughter, she had been exposed to calculations of prudence versus contingency, as well as to the idea of self-protection's limits, all her life.

Two days later, Michael paid another visit to Irving. With Lee not around, Ruth was free to show him a copy of the letter. Michael detected her concern, but when she approached him, he was reading magazines and didn't want to be bothered. He looked at the salutation, and instead of seeing "Dear Sirs" saw what looked like a woman's name—"Dear Lisa." A glance at the contents didn't impress him. If Lee had been to Mexico, what difference did it make? And the rest only appeared to be some sort of "strutting," or fantasy, which he'd seen evidence of in Oswald before.*

The most useful thing Michael Paine could have done at this moment was to tell his wife exactly what sort of strutting he'd seen Lee perform. "I talked quite a lot with Ruth," he says today, recalling the general state of his marriage, "because I didn't mind what I said. I didn't mind the possibility of losing her, or

---

*Some conspiracy-minded researchers have expressed suspicion over how Ruth's handwritten duplication of Oswald's letter "has never surfaced." In fact, it exists, carefully preserved among papers she donated to the Friends Historical Library at Swarthmore College.

something like that. I used to think we talked very freely, and now I think there must have been a lot of things we didn't talk about, probably. I don't know for sure." Without question, this was a time Ruth *needed* him to talk, to apply his intelligent, if distinctly odd, mind to the subject of this problematical young man in their midst. But she could not get him to do it. If Michael's conduct was never, in the language of Texas divorce law, "unkind, cruel, harsh and tyrannical," it was, in this instance, maddeningly indifferent. Ruth had to content herself with thinking she could still show the letter to Agent Hosty, whom she had come to trust, when he next paid a visit.

Hosty, however, did not return to the house during the next ten days, and Oswald himself stayed away from Irving until Thursday, November 21. He followed his routine of working at the Book Depository, watching TV at the rooming house, and reading a day-old newspaper when he found one lying about. Meanwhile, Marina and Ruth resumed their maternal round and got ready for Lynn's fourth-birthday party. On the subject of gifts, Ruth told her companion that she did not believe in buying toy guns for her children, and that she wished more people would think about this issue. Marina did not reply, but it was she who suggested to Lee that he not come out to the Paines' during the weekend of November 16: He had, after all, just been there for the three-day weekend that included Veterans' Day, and with the children's party going on he would only add to the commotion. The weekend after that should be less hectic.

Part Two   November 22, 1963

# One

"I have no recollection of him at all on the morning of November 22nd, except an empty coffee cup." Lee had made himself some instant and left the cup in the sink. Ruth never heard him shower or close the door when he departed the house to catch a ride to the Book Depository with Linnie Mae Randle's brother.

Marina Oswald, typically the last adult to awaken at 2515 West Fifth, remained asleep while Ruth, in the living room, prepared to watch television coverage of the President's chamber of commerce breakfast at the Hotel Texas. One camera focused on the dais, another on a doorway. Awaiting Kennedy's arrival, the WFAA reporter vamped through some history about a day in 1901:

*President William McKinley was appearing at the Pan-American Exposition in Buffalo, New York, and at a public reception the crowd moved in around him, and the three Secret Service men who were guarding him had no chance to screen the people approaching him. Because it was a hot day, the Secret Service also allowed people to have handkerchiefs in their hands to wipe their perspiring brows. It just so happened that one of the thousands of handkerchiefs in the large hall covered a revolver in the hand of 28-year-old Leon Czolgosz. He was an unemployed mill-*

*worker. He said he was an anarchist. He also was a man with a long history of mental illness, and as in so many important occasions of the world no one seemed to sense that anything different was going to happen . . .*

At 9:10, John F. Kennedy entered the picture. Ruth, after a brief glimpse of him, realized the time and hurried Lynn off to her 9:15 appointment with the dentist, Dr. Lollar. Knowing that Marina would enjoy the spectacle of the Kennedys arriving in Dallas, even if she couldn't understand the newscaster's English, Ruth left the television on when she drove off from the house.

There were, of course, errands to run after the dentist, and she didn't return home until almost noon, at which time she found the divorce petition, posted from downtown the night before, in her mailbox. Over in Fort Worth, at Bell Helicopter, the other party to it, Michael Paine, was getting ready for an early lunch in the cafeteria attached to a nearby bowling alley. Part of his conversation with Dave Noel, a young colleague, would involve "the character of assassins . . . of all things." It was Michael who brought the subject up, though he and Noel soon realized they lacked "enough historical knowledge" to get very far with it. As topics go, Michael would later concede the peculiarity of this one, "unless you believe in extrasensory perception," the way his stepfather Arthur Young did.

The TV camera lost sight of the President's motorcade after its departure from Love Field. There would be nothing much to see until Kennedy's 12:30 speech at the Trade Mart, and so, during the gap, Ruth went into the kitchen to prepare lunch. Once again, she left the television on.

When the bulletin came, her reaction was immediate: *That's it for Texas. I'm going back to Philadelphia.*

Like most politically aware people, Ruth Paine, upon first hearing the news, believed that the shooting of John F. Kennedy had been committed by a right-wing extremist. She belonged as well to a smaller group who instantly sensed that their own lives would be altered by the deed, and to a much smaller category still, a handful of people she didn't yet know she had joined, ones whose lives had just been stopped, like watches in a bomb blast.

For another couple of hours, Ruth's apprehension, and then grief, remained ordinary, the sort an additional million people began to share each minute. Allowing Lynn to help, she lit some candles, explaining to Marina, to whom she'd translated the bulletin, that this was her own way of praying. She knew Marina understood the religious impulse in a way that would have disgusted her husband. Last year Marina had gotten Junie baptized without telling Lee first, and had shown Ruth the baptismal certificate during one of her friend's visits to Neely Street.

Even now, entering the limbo hour that Kennedy lay in Parkland Hospital, the maternal workday went on. Marina stepped into the backyard to hang laundry. Ruth soon joined her there with further news from the television: The shots fired at the motorcade were now thought to have come from the Texas School Book Depository. Lee, presumably, would have quite a story to tell when he arrived back here tonight.*

Without explanation, Marina allowed Ruth to finish hanging the clothes, while she herself went back into the house and then, taking care not to be seen, the garage. She was suddenly mindful of a secret she had been keeping *with* Lee, not from him. She checked to see that the blanket roll remained where she'd last noticed it a few weeks ago. To her relief, the bundle appeared to be in the same place and condition.

Soon after, while the two women sat on the couch in front of the TV, Ruth had to translate the news that John F. Kennedy was dead. She and Marina exchanged thoughts of what an awful fate had just befallen Jacqueline Kennedy and her two children. Marina, despite her trip to the garage, had not shed all fears that her violent, assassination-prone husband might yet prove in-

---

*Ruth's conveyance of this information to Marina has seemed suspicious to a number of conspiracy theorists, beginning with Mark Lane (*Rush to Judgment*, 1966). If Ruth mistakenly believed, as she would later testify, that Oswald worked in *another* warehouse owned by the TSBD, not the one at the corner of Elm and Houston where Kennedy was hit, why would she have gone out to Marina with this piece of news? "Why not?" Ruth responds today. "It doesn't mystify me." The two TSBD buildings were not far apart. Oswald "could easily have walked over, or whatever." At the least, as part of the same organization, "he would hear what was going on."

Those unsatisfied with Ruth on this point ignore the fact that she could easily have been duplicitous, saying she believed all along that Oswald worked in the building where the sniper's nest was found. She volunteered the anomaly to authorities.

volved in this catastrophe. She apologized for not crying, a reticence that Ruth attributed to personality, not preoccupation.

The two women continued watching television, abandoning their plan to go shopping for shoes with the $10 Lee had recently given Marina. Then there was a knock at the door. Ruth answered it and discovered a whole group of law-enforcement officers, including men from the Dallas County sheriff's department. She surmised that they were there to serve papers in connection with the divorce, until one of them announced that Oswald was in custody for shooting a policeman. When the officers asked to come in, she managed to inquire if they had a warrant. They didn't, but assured her they could get one right away. She did not pursue the point: "That's okay," she said, "we're all upset. Come on in."*

Ruth thought "they'd come in and sit on my sofa and talk to me." Instead, "six guys spread out all over the house right away, like water." They asked whether Lee owned a gun, and Ruth said no. She then translated the question to Marina, using the Russian word for "long gun" because that was the only one she knew.

Yes, Marina responded, to Ruth's astonishment; Lee did have a gun. Marina then led the way to the garage.

No mention had yet been made of John Kennedy, only of a murdered patrolman, but Ruth now understood what this was really about.

*One assassination legend has Ruth greeting the officers with the words "Come in, we've been expecting you." She firmly denies this today: "I was not expecting them, and I did not say that."

Asked nearly forty years later to reconstruct what happened in the garage, she groans before obliging:

"[Marina] showed this blanket roll, which was on the floor. The officer picked it up, folded it over his arm. It was empty. He didn't even have to open it. You could see it was empty. That was when I had this feeling, 'My God, it could have been Lee.' That he came out last night, that the gun had been there . . . That was probably the worst moment. . . ."

Within minutes, still warrantless, the police were hauling off box after box of the Paines' and Oswalds' belongings, ignoring Ruth's protests. A neighbor, Dorothy Roberts, watching this front-lawn drama that must have resembled an eviction, thought she had never seen Mrs. Paine so angry. The enormity unfolding—in her house, in the world—was still too new for sensible, calibrated reactions. If the seizure of Ruth's 78-rpm folk-dance records made little sense, her complaint—that she needed them for a class next weekend—might have seemed, had there been even a moment to reflect, wildly moot. When an officer ordered that she and Marina get ready to go with the police, Ruth remembers preparing "to walk around the house to where the babysitters were," to hire them for the rest of the afternoon. "I started out the door, and one of the officers started with me, and I said, 'Oh, you don't have to come!' And then I thought, Oh, yes he does! Of course he does!"

One policeman grabbed Ruth's arm, and another threatened to take her children "to Juvenile" if she didn't hurry. She turned to her daughter and said, with deliberate evenness, "Lynn, you may go with us." Neither of them went anywhere until baby-sitters were found for Chris. Once downtown, Ruth would further irritate the police when, before signing the affidavit they composed from her oral statements, she corrected its English. At the police station, inside a file case seized from the garage, rested a college essay in which young Ruth Hyde had mused: "I don't act like a rebel very much, but I have always enjoyed a great deal of personal freedom and find I bristle and rally forces of resistance when it is taken away."

Even so, from the first hours of this first afternoon, it is Ruth's open-faced cooperation that stands out. As the police car headed from Irving to Dallas, an officer in the front seat wheeled around to ask her: "Are you a Communist?"

"No," she replied, "and I don't even feel the need of the Fifth Amendment on that one."

She remembers translating the question to Marina, who, sitting beside her in the back of the police car, was "very quiet at that point," and "not just because of the language difficulty."

Having escaped from the Book Depository—surely to his own amazement—Lee Oswald took a bus and taxi back to his rooming house in Oak Cliff, where he picked up the pistol he used minutes later to kill the patrolman, J. D. Tippit, who stopped him near the corner of Tenth and Patton. Ducking into the Texas Theatre without a ticket, Oswald was finally captured during a double feature of *War Is Hell* and *Cry of Battle*, the sort of combat movies Lee liked to stay up watching on the Paines' TV.

Neither Ruth nor Michael saw him in the city jail above the police station on Friday night. Ruth remained taken up with Marina's needs, particularly translation, no matter what new

suspicions she might be entitled to entertain about her companion. And as the world's press began clamoring outside the
Police and Courts Building, the Paines were about to become involved with the rest of Lee's family.

Oswald's older brother Robert, a straight-arrow sales coordi-
nator for the Acme Brick Company, had done a remarkable job
transcending the difficulties of his early life, but as Ruth remembers, he was "instantly turned off" by his new acquaintances. Robert would later recall the encounter in a book:
Michael Paine's "handshake was weak, and his eyes were cold,
unfeeling, almost expressionless. I felt that he was not looking
at me but was staring straight through me." Robert's estimate of
Ruth managed to be nearly the opposite but no more favorable:
"I felt that she was stimulated by the drama of the moment and
her rapid comments to everyone who would listen struck me as
almost boastful: 'I've had them over at my house,' she would say
to anyone who did not seem to recognize how close she had been
to the center of the tragedy."

This exaggerated behavior actually involved Ruth's natural
tendency to *cooperate*—with almost anyone, in whatever circumstances, including the adversarial and bizarre. The sense of
being trespassed upon, during the illegal seizures this afternoon, had been replaced here at the police station by a desire,
overstimulated though it may have been, to assist, explain, and
conciliate. People not used to the sight of Ruth's shoulder put
gaily to the wheel—girlish exuberance and nervous, high laughter dart in and out of her manner and conversation, even when
the prevailing mood is grave—would have found her behavior
even odder than Michael's apparently cool composure. But the

extreme situation was only making each one more like himself. That afternoon, when the police went about their roughshod business, Ruth had begun "to realize that they had no clue . . . what kind of people we were." But the Dallas police, and Robert Oswald, knew for sure that the Paines were very odd characters for these parts. And what twelve hours ago looked eccentric now seemed decidedly sinister.

Much of what Lee's brother had overcome in life was present on the police station's third floor Friday night, in the threnodic person of his mother, Marguerite, whose hands ceaselessly wrung themselves over what she insisted had been a life much misunderstood and undercompensated. Ruth would come to see Lee Oswald as very much his mother's son, though she did not yet know that the strongest bond between him and Robert had been forged during the long-ago time when Marguerite, too put-upon to care for her sons, had placed them in an orphanage. Ruth might be as much this woman's opposite as nature could fashion, but tonight the suspected assassin's mother was one more Oswald to be assisted. Marguerite was invited back to Irving to have supper and spend the night.

West Fifth Street showed few signs of disturbance when the Paines arrived home with the Oswald women around 9:00. *Life* magazine was briefly on the scene, to take some pictures and make an appointment for tomorrow, but the news media, barely yet known by that term, were otherwise not much in evidence. The important reporting venues were still downtown—the murder scene and police headquarters—and the presence being craved was Oswald's own. Michael went out to a drive-in for a bag of hamburgers. Ruth and Marina got the four children bedded down before beginning to converse in the kitchen. Marina finally told Ruth how, last night, Lee had asked her to live with him again, once he found an apartment. He'd pledged to get one right away if she said yes.

Today Ruth remembers wondering whether this apartment discussion meant that Lee had wanted to put Marina in a location "where she wouldn't be immediately available to the public. And yet there would have been absolutely no way of getting an apartment that night. So nothing makes sense is I guess what I'm saying." Oswald had left Marina almost all his money—$170 in the bureau—but why bother making this protective gesture, Ruth asks, when "the basic act was so damaging"?* That night the questions were coming too quickly to complete themselves, let alone yield answers, and inside Ruth's mind they began to strike a wall of wholly unfamiliar material: a desire for retribution.

After 10:00 p.m. Robert Oswald was driving west on Highway 80, without the radio, trying to collect his emotions while his car raced over the flat road beneath the stars. But the immensity of Texas was useless to the eight people crammed inside the Paines' tiny house. Marguerite was already proving a difficult guest: She had been annoyed by the *Life* photographer, whose lens had caught her with her stockings rolled down, and was peeved at the apparent centrality of Marina and Ruth to this event, when she, as people seemed to forget, was the mother. She had not finished figuring out how she could turn this major occurrence into the money-making opportunity that had always

---

*"He never struck you as being a negligent father?" I asked Ruth in June 2000. "That's correct," she replied, "except for this major event! He could hardly have hurt the family more than by assassinating the President."

eluded her. Where, she asked loudly, were the lawyers? "If we were important people, they would be coming to the door to offer legal counsel." A thought more conclusive than most others formed in Ruth's swirling mind: "This lady sees herself as a victim. Nobody's going to treat her right. She doesn't *expect* to be treated right." Marguerite, in turn, saw Ruth's excited obliging of the *Life* man as a craving for attention—perhaps the single point of agreement Mrs. Oswald would experience with her son Robert.*

Ruth's last waking thoughts on November 22 were, in fact, far from self-regarding. Inside the back bedroom with only Lynn and Chris, she remembers telling herself: "You know, you've really got to get to sleep. Don't obsess about this. You've got to sleep . . ." Her main worry was "how can I make this as easy for my children as possible?" Her father, Bill Hyde, had earlier tonight started for Texas, flying from Columbus to Chicago, but had turned back at O'Hare when his daughter assured him, over the telephone, that there was no point in coming down.

Ruth succeeded in falling asleep while, on the other side of the wall, in the bigger bedroom, Marina quietly showed Marguerite, the mother-in-law she hadn't seen in a year, two photo-

---

*Ruth's only misstep, as she made clear to the Warren Commission, was in trying to please everybody at once: "I made the mistake I now think of turning on another light simply as an act of hostess, it was dim in the living room but I hadn't realized until later that I was making it possible for [the photographer] to take a picture.

"I didn't know what was best for me to do as hostess. It seemed to me that Mrs. Oswald, Sr., Mrs. Marguerite Oswald, was both interested in encouraging the Life Magazine representatives and still didn't really want her picture taken. . . ."

graphs just extracted from Junie's baby book. They depicted, not Marina's eldest daughter, but Lee, in back of the Neely Street apartment, brandishing a rifle, a pistol, and two Communist newspapers, *The Militant* and *The Worker*. She had taken the pictures herself, back in March, at his insistence.

Marguerite now implored her, with gestures, to keep the photos away from Ruth. Tomorrow, while visiting Lee in jail, Marina would hide them in her shoe. Later she would burn them, not knowing Oswald had been sufficiently proud of the pose to make numerous prints at the graphic-arts firm where he then worked. The police would have a set that had been with his things in the garage.

No one in the house knew what revelations and dangers might lie ahead. At his Friday-night press conference, Oswald's smirk was inflaming a local vigilantism that might be a matter of guilty overcompensation but still had to be reckoned with. Between developments, newscasters were beginning to locate, and create, parallels between the killings of Kennedy and Abraham Lincoln, whose funeral was at this hour being researched, at Jacqueline Kennedy's request, by flashlight-carrying aides in the stacks of the Library of Congress. Not far from there, Mrs. Mary Surratt's boarding house, where John Wilkes Booth had been an occasional presence in the early months of 1865, still housed a handful of Washingtonians. When detectives had searched it on the weekend of Lincoln's assassination, they found that Mrs. Surratt's daughter, Anna, had hidden a daguerreotype of Booth behind a picture called *Morning, Noon, and Night*. Anna's legal peril was never very great, but within three months her mother would become the first woman ever hanged by the federal government, on the basis of some shaky testimony about her connection to "shooting irons" involved in the crime committed by her occasional guest.

# Two

Robert Oswald saw his brother in the Dallas city jail on Saturday afternoon. His searching look into Lee's eyes prompted the accused assassin to say, "Brother, you won't find anything there."

Their brief conversation, reconstructed by Robert a few years later, soon turned to the Paines:

> "Well, what about Marina?" I asked [Lee]. "What do you think she's going to do now, with those two kids?"
>
> "My friends will take care of them," he said.
>
> "Do you mean the Paines?" I asked.
>
> "Yes," he said, indicating by his reaction that he was a little surprised that I knew of the Paines.
>
> Although I had met them for the first time the previous night at the Dallas police station, I already had strong reservations about Michael and Ruth Paine—particularly about Michael.
>
> "I don't think they're any friends of yours," I said.
>
> "Yes, they are."
>
> "Well, they're sure not any friends of mine."

On the last full day of his life, Lee continued to make use of his benefactors. He even involved four-year-old Lynn Paine in the construction of an alibi, telling the police he'd broken his pattern and come out to Irving on a Thursday because Ruth was giving a birthday party for her daughter this weekend, and he didn't want to be in the way. Should Ruth tell them that the party had in fact taken place the previous weekend, Lee—as Jean Davison sees it, in her book *Oswald's Game*—"could say he had simply misunderstood. As so often happened, Oswald was twisting the truth to fit his own purposes—it was almost as though he saw reality itself as nothing more than raw material to be shaped and used."

He saw Ruth similarly. On Saturday afternoon he called the house and asked her to contact John Abt, a left-wing defense lawyer in New York. Even Ruth had her limits, or nearly so; she was astonished by Oswald's crust in asking a favor of someone whose life he had just flung toward chaos and infamy. Still, she tried, albeit without success, to reach the attorney: "If I'd been smarter," she says today, "I'd have said to him he needs somebody *now*. Get a temporary guy. Didn't think of that."

Lee called again around 9:30 that night. The last words Ruth would ever hear from him were a request to speak with Marina, but she had to tell him that his wife had left that morning with his mother, a translator, and Tommy Thompson from *Life* magazine. Oswald then complained that Marina should be available to him. So, Ruth remembers, she

called the hotel and asked for Tommy Thompson's room, and Marguerite Oswald answered the phone. So I said,

"Well, I'd like to talk to Marina." "Well, no, you can't talk to Marina." And I said, "Well, Lee has called me and he wants to be able to reach her, and he doesn't know how to do that." And she said, "Well, we really can't be too concerned about what Lee thinks at this point." And that was pretty much the end of the conversation.*

Personal legal jeopardy seems scarcely to have crossed Ruth's mind. She never retained a lawyer for herself, and it was mostly out of curiosity that she asked FBI agent Bardwell Odum whether her phone line was now tapped. She recalls him saying, " 'Mrs. Paine, you *answer* the questions we have; why would we put a tap on your line?' " She "let it go at that, which was not good enough, you know. He didn't answer the question. So my guess is, yes, that they tapped the line. But I wasn't worrying about it . . . I saw it as part of their job."

During the weekend of the assassination, Ruth's only real concern about the phone involved good manners. "I'll tell you what I did do," she says with a laugh. "There we were in Irving, and we had a two-party telephone line . . . and it wasn't that we heard the other party, but when we were on the line, they couldn't use it, and vice versa. So, along about Sunday, or maybe it could have been Saturday or Monday, I called the phone company and said I would like to make a change in the service. She said, 'Oh, you want an unlisted number!' I said, 'No, no, I'd just

*Marguerite was thinking way ahead of everyone else. Had the assassination taken place in today's quick-kill communications culture, she would by Saturday morning have had a media advisor sorting through fruit baskets arriving from Barbara Walters and Larry King.

like to have a line just for us, because I think the other party is not getting much use of his phone.' So they did that right away."*

Ruth today acknowledges the naivete involved in failing to consider the possibility of her own arrest. A kind of willed obliviousness was also operating. She remembers what she did when the police returned on Saturday, with a warrant:

> I was on my way to the grocery store . . . and at that point I was feeding apples to newsmen, too—a lot of folks comin' through. And I didn't want to be *bothered?* I didn't want it to interrupt my life, so I went ahead to the grocery store, leaving my home untended to the Dallas police, which was

---

*Someone from the phone company may have engaged in their own eaves-dropping. Agent Hosty, in his book on the case, describes a by-now much-discussed call from Lyman Paine to his son Michael: "A long-distance operator, completely of her own volition, had illegally listened in on the conversation and later reported what she had heard to the FBI. [Lyman] Paine was a well-known Trotskyite, and during his telephone call to his son, he said, 'We all know who did this,' and told his son to be careful. We at the FBI interpreted that comment to mean that [Lyman] was speculating that the Soviet KGB had carried out the assassination, just as Stalin had the KGB assassinate his political rival Leon Trotsky."

There are different versions of this phone call—some put it on the 22nd, others on the 23rd; Ruth has even "heard it ascribed to Michael, that it was a call I received from [him]."

Conspiracy theorists place a sinister construction upon the call, whereas probability tells one that Lyman Paine, like people across the political spectrum, was advancing his own armchair theory about who might be behind the assassination. He was unusual only in knowing someone close enough to the events whom he might reasonably tell to be "careful"—of, presumably, reporters, the police and vigilantes.

bizarre, to say the least . . . *That* was not smart, or not appropriate, but it didn't hurt me.

She would soon, during some of those errands, have Michael
to watch the house. If she was about to lose Marina—first to *Life*
magazine and then the authorities—Ruth was regaining her husband. Michael stood ready to move back in, for the sake of solidarity during such a dangerous time, and for an immediate,
practical reason: his landlady wanted him out of the Villa Fon-
taine apartments in Grand Prairie. Knowing his connection to
the assassin, the other residents, he remembers, "were out-
raged that I should continue to live there," even if they "didn't
love Kennedy nearly as much as I did."

Agent Hosty also returned to West Fifth Street on Saturday
morning. Ruth welcomed any shift in responsibility for the case
away from the Dallas police toward the more professional FBI,
and Jim Hosty's regard for her would remain high in the months
and years to come. But he now picked up "negative vibes" from
her spouse, who had been edgy enough to call the Irving police
and request round-the-clock guarding of the house. The request was denied, but four decades later, informed of this protective, husbandly gesture, Ruth says, "Oh, really?" sounding
distinctly pleased.

The police may have blocked off the street, which Ruth remembers as still being remarkably "calm and quiet." That would
change, briefly, just before noon on Sunday, when Jack Ruby
shot Oswald during his transfer to the Dallas county jail. Ruth
was sitting on the couch, watching developments on the television that stood near the large front picture window. Through it,

she could observe an Irving police vehicle. Suddenly she noticed an officer

> get out of his car, go to the trunk and get out a long gun, a rifle, and come in toward the house. And he wanted to come in; I said he could come in, and he proceeded to close the curtains on this one large window at the front; and there were two in the back—I mean, this is a real open house—and he closed those and he peeked out . . . He clearly had gotten a message to come in and protect Mrs. Paine and see who else was going to be killed off

—either by vigilantes or fellow conspirators. Ruth hoped this new disturbance wouldn't wake Chris and Lynn, who were down for their naps; she soon persuaded the policeman to reopen the curtains.

Before Oswald was pronounced dead, Marina called from the hotel. The Secret Service was taking her into protective custody. Would Ruth assemble some things she needed for herself and the baby? Not a word about Lee was exchanged. Marina, who had by now destroyed the rifle photo she had never shown Ruth, was passing out of her charitable friend's life. The weird impersonality of the telephone conversation amounted only to an exaggeration of the distance the Russian woman had actually been keeping all along.

And yet Ruth still tended to see Marina, not Kennedy, as the catastrophe's ground zero.

For all the Gandhian "soul force" she liked to apply against violence, Ruth Paine could not keep from feeling glad that Lee

Oswald was dead. Not from her anger with him, but via a line of reasoning that ran parallel to Jack Ruby's. He had decided that, with Oswald out of the way, Jacqueline Kennedy would not have to return to Dallas for a trial; Ruth believed that Lee's disappearance from the scene would make things easier for Marina. She never gave a thought to going to Oswald's funeral, until she learned, afterwards, that his wife had had no one to translate the service for her.

Ruth, of course, would not truly have willed such a violent end to Lee—in fact, had Oswald survived to explain himself, there might have been, over the years, fewer questions and suspicions about her own life. But Ruth doubts he would ever have confessed. Intrigued by his calm in front of the cameras, she still marvels, and laughs, over his televised explanation ("A policeman hit me") for the bruise above his eye. "Really!" she exclaims. "Victim that he is!" She suspects "he would have been losing reality more and more" had Ruby not put an end to him. "We don't know what would have happened over time, but I think he would have fallen apart," even gone "full-blown psychotic," though "psychotic implies that he would *really* lose reality. I think he would tend to know that he was lying. So that's not a total loss of reality. It's just not dishing up reality to the people around you."*

*Ruth still believes that Oswald may not have decided to shoot the President until Thursday, the 21st, during his workday at the Book Depository. Had he taken the decision earlier, he would likely have carried his pistol to work that day, knowing he couldn't return to his rooming house that night—not while he was depending on a ride out to Irving with Linnie Mae Randle's brother to pick up the more-important rifle.

At no time before his death, despite what calamity he brought upon her, did Ruth ever lose sight of Oswald's rights. She made the call to John Abt and, along with Michael, refrained from giving any television interview until after Lee was dead. "I think it's a terrible thing to judge a man before he's brought to trial," she then told the ABC reporter, "and in this case it's a very difficult thing not to do, the evidence was so incriminating . . . I began to wonder how they ever could get a jury that would give him an impartial trial, but now, of course, he's dead—he's been, in effect, judged quickly and hanged." In a fuzzy overduplicated video of this interview, Ruth sits on the living room couch beside a big decanter-shaped lamp, an old-fashioned microphone looped around her neck. Looking well-groomed but exhausted —the doorbell is still ringing during the segment—she tells the reporter she "was surprised to learn [Lee] had a gun," and that she never imagined him as fanatical or dangerous. Prone to self-victimization, yes; but she had hoped that, eventually, "he might find that life was generous."

Her own sense that life is like that may have saved her in the days to follow. Today, Ruth reflects: "I think of people this kind of catastrophic event could happen to, I'm probably better off than most, because I feel the world is a kindly place and it'll treat me okay, that there may be chaos around, but I'll come out okay." By Sunday night, she had already begun to get encouraging phone calls from people in her life, and similar letters were on the way. The Laceys, whom she'd been visiting at the time of the Birmingham bombing, wrote to ask if she wouldn't like to come back to Richmond, Indiana, for a while; an old friend in Cambridge, Massachusetts, saw the TV interviews and just wanted the Paines to know how proud she'd been to observe "first Ruth then Michael coming through in the Emersonian tradition, via the ABC network. . . ."

At Antioch, Ruth had written about wanting "to throw light into whatever blind spots . . . have been hiding something I have been afraid to face." But sometimes it was the light itself that blinded her. In these early postassassination days, others took better note of the dangers. Her brother, Carl Hyde, worried about her safety, as did her mother-in-law, Mrs. Young, who feared, upon hearing Oswald had been shot, "that some wild person would take a shot at you and Michael for having sheltered the Russian wife."*

Ruth responded to the sympathetic letters, and when an anonymous piece of hate mail arrived in mid-December—*Madam Paine; You touch me deeply right where I sit about the hog wash on the Oswald family. You seem to know very little about your bed partners. The rot of Dallas stinks far and wide . . . It is always easy to put on a front but it is not so easy now that all of you have to live with a fact*—she marked the envelope with a note that this letter, at least so far, stood apart from all the others. Even so, in the weeks approaching Christmas, Ruth recalls how she "reserved time for myself when [Lynn and Chris] were both asleep in the afternoon to try to read the paper, and I'd end up crying all the time."

She waited for things to get better, and particularly for the resumption of her friendship with Marina.

---

*By the next weekend, Michael himself decided things were sufficiently back to normal that he *could* go to that folk-dance conference; and he did.

# Three

On Thanksgiving Day, November 28, Mrs. Arthur Young wrote her daughter-in-law to express relief over how "the Secret Service had taken the poor girl off your hands." Still, Mrs. Young remained distressed by the persistent emotional connection between Ruth and Marina and, more particularly, the public's association of the two women.

Her letter scolds Ruth for "being very unrealistic in even thinking of taking Marina to Paoli [PA] or anywhere. I feel you are being carried along on a kind of idealism that is beyond common sense." Her daughter-in-law needs to "simmer down," to realize that her

> responsibility to Marina is over and quietly remove yourself from the public eye and ear, [or] you will unnecessarily tie yourself, the children and Michael for life to a most disgraceful and horrible event. People will forget your part was innocent and that you offered help in true Quaker fashion. They will be confused about the details but just remember you were connected in some way.

Most dangerous of all, from Mrs. Young's point of view, is the impression in the newspapers that Ruth has spared no "thought to the enormity of the loss of Kennedy," but only to Marina's plight. Even if that is all the reporters ask her about, Ruth needs to consider how her replies sound: "I think in Texas you are not aware that people are still crying," writes Mrs. Young, who tries to sound more urgent than harsh.*

Ruth was grimly aware that some Texans' satisfaction with Kennedy's murder might actually have limited the number of local threats made against her. But Mrs. Young's warnings were hardly unreasonable. Quoted statements from Ruth in an article like one that ran in the *New York World-Telegram* still sound strangely blithe and disproportionate, even if they really just amount to Ruth speaking simple truths without guile or filtration:

> "I was so pleased to have my own resident Russian tutor living in the house with me," Mrs. Paine mused. "And shocked that my interest became so tangled in world affairs."

Ruth had agreed to write an article for *Look*—a very bad idea, thought Mrs. Young—in the hope that it would help people take a sympathetic view of Marina. "I love [her] as if she were a sister," says a surviving ghostwritten draft not nearly so well composed as what Ruth might have produced herself. The piece concludes: "I want the nation to know what an innocent, fine person [Marina] is. *If only* I can somehow do this, perhaps she can bring up her fatherless children in a place where they don't have to lock

*Ruth's own mother, Carol Hyde, had written her daughter on November 26 to offer Marina "the use of my home, rent free, for the winter, if it seems appropriate."

the front door at night." Which is to say, a place like her own house.

In the end, Ruth was not unhappy to have the piece killed by *Look*'s editors. She today recognizes how excessive her preoccupation with Marina must have looked, and recalls the shocked appearance of a *New York Times* reporter when, after Lee's death, she told him, 'Well, at least Marina won't have to testify." Even Congressman Gerald Ford, after serving on the Warren Commission, expressed concern about how "Ruth's anxieties over Marina's well-being would create another plot theory which, when added to all the rest, became a spider's nest of apparent machinations."

As things turned out, Ruth's worries and efforts were largely beside the point. The country showed itself spontaneously well-disposed toward Marina Oswald—in part, perhaps, to prove how "big" it was by bear-hugging this pretty daughter of the Soviet enemy. It seems unlikely that an American wife of Oswald would have inspired the same quantity of good wishes and money that soon began flowing to Marina. A seventeen-year-old girl from Albuquerque would address a note to her in care of, simply, "Mrs. Paine, Irving, Texas," and it would get there, telling the assassin's widow: "I feel sorry and sad not only for the president but for you."

When Secret Service agents came to West Fifth Street to retrieve Lee's wedding ring—left behind on the morning of November 22 in a cup that had belonged to Marina's grandmother—Ruth also turned over the first of the checks and cash donations that had begun accumulating for her former guest. Various Friends' congregations across the U.S., hearing of Marina's connection to a fellow Quaker, started sending money to the Meeting in Dallas. The National Council of Churches of Christ passed a resolution calling for prayers on behalf of Marina and her family, and expressing "deepest appreciation to those who ministered to Mrs. Oswald's immediate personal and spiritual needs, thus not leaving the Church without a measure of Christian witness."

But Marina's personal needs were rapidly changing. Ruth might faithfully return to Parkland Hospital to donate the second pint of blood the women had pledged in exchange for Rachel's low-cost delivery, but her help now also involved such things as forwarding interview requests, sometimes for $10,000, from the London *Daily Express* or *Stern*.

Ruth saw several reasons to decline invitations to get away from Irving. She wanted to keep things as routine seeming as possible for Chris and Lynn, and she thought she should be available to "answer legitimate questions that came to the door." Yet as much as anything else, it was "to solve this mystery of Marina" that she remained. Where exactly was her friend? Still at the Inn of the Six Flags in Fort Worth, where the Secret Service had taken her on November 24? What were Marina's plans? And, most important, did she know her rights?

Early attempts to communicate with Marina were passed through the Irving police, and they received no answer. "I am afraid," Ruth wrote,

that you never want to see me again. It is true, we have horrible memories. It is probably better that we do not live together again. But we are sisters, whether we want to be or not. Sisters in misfortune. I want to see you sometime. For now, it is probably better that I do not know where you are. I would like to know though whether you are with Mother Oswald or not. In my opinion, it would be difficult to live with her.

Ruth still remembers her uncertainty and sense of rejection. "That was a terrible time." Marina "could have written me a letter saying back off, in response to my several letters asking how things are going. She never did that. She finally sent a Christmas card [with] zero content."

In fact, the card was worse than nothing at all. "You wrote me," Ruth responded, "as if I were an old grandmother and not a friend. You closed your face to me. Is it true, have I offended you? If so, excuse, forgive me, please. I did not want to offend and do not wish to. But I am coarse and stupid, especially in Russian." This painful self-abasement, so much that of the baffled, discarded lover, extends to Ruth's reiteration of how Marina's presence in Irving was never a matter of charity. "How many times have I said when you were here, that I was giving nothing more than I received. You never understood how useful it was to me to speak Russian every day." She is now trying to persuade Marina of what she'd once hoped to convince Lee.

Guessing correctly, in part from the postmark on the Christmas card, that Marina might be staying with her new business manager, James Martin, and his wife, in Grand Prairie,* Ruth

*Martin had been manager of the Inn of the Six Flags prior to seeing new opportunities in the future of his famous guest.

hand delivered the above letter on the afternoon of December
27. She brought along three recipes, a hair dryer Marina had
left behind, and more of the checks still arriving at 2515 West
Fifth. She consulted Marina's lawyer, John Thorne, of Thorne &
Leach—a bad-joke legal name that she can laugh over today—
"about the fact that the checks that I wrote to Marina to transfer
cash money that had come to me for her were coming back with
someone else's handwriting on the back. And he was absolutely
unhelpful. 'If Marina wants to contact you, she will contact you
directly.' "

Week after week, Ruth's pleas continued:

December 28: They say that it is your choice to speak with
someone or not to speak. That is, if you
want to see me they *then* would give me
permission to meet with you. But I do not
believe this, while I have not heard it from
your lips. For that reason I bother you and
want a refusal from you and not only from
Secret Service.

January 3: I want to invite you to come to my house to
have supper or lunch on Tuesday the 7th,
Wednesday the 8th or Thursday the 9th . . .
Possibly, someone has said to you that it is
better not to see me. Perhaps they think
that I will find out and will tell where you
are now living. They don't know that I am a
truthful person and that if I say I will not

tell something—I do not. But you know that
I am honest. You can ask me not to speak
about something and I will not. Not even to
Michael if you prefer. But in general I
don't want to know anything except that
you are free, that you know your rights. At
first I did not expect to see you, as I knew
that Secret Service, F.B.I. wanted to ask
you many questions. But [it is] already six
weeks since the killing of the president. It
is time for you to rest.

She encloses pre-assassination pictures of Junie, new ones of
Chris. A week later, with the desperate attenuation of the jilted,
she says she's even willing to keep writing without response.

January 10: If you are not against it, I will write you
regularly, and when it is convenient to you
I want to speak and chat with you. You
know that I have no better friend in Texas
than you. I talk with Dorothy (neighbor)
and Mrs. Craig, but we are not close. It is
not like with my friends in Philadelphia
and with you . . . I will write you in a week.

On January 6, Ruth gets Greg Olds, President of the Dallas
Civil Liberties Union, to inquire of Martin, the FBI, Thorne,
and the Secret Service about Marina's status. Through her protective retinue, Marina issues a reply, assuring the DCLU that

she does not require their help; that she is grateful for the Secret Service's protection; and that while she considers Ruth "one of my best friends," now is not the time to see her: "When I feel I'm ready, I would with pleasure like to see Mrs Ruth Paine, who is a very nice person. I hope you understand I lived in a stranger's house and I would not want to inconvenience anyone as kind as Mrs Ruth Paine with visitors I be sure to receive and also I give much time to visits with the FBI." *The New York Times,* reporting the exchange on January 11, 1964 ("Oswald's Widow Rebuffs Liberties Union"), has Marina calling 2515 West Fifth a "strange" house instead of a "stranger's."

However sensitive she claimed to be toward Ruth's comfort, Marina still made no effort to get back in touch. But Ruth persisted:

January 23:  I requested a new Sears Roebuck catalog for you (Spring–Summer). I have it here at home. I also have some glass (baby) bottles and your bath powder. If you wish these things say so, and I will bring them to Martin's home or to Thorne's office, whatever is more convenient. But perhaps we will soon see each other. I hope so. I think that after you have seen President Johnson's Commission you can see me more easily. Is that so?

February 3:  I saw your interview on television. You have learned a lot of English. From this

(TV) appearance all will know (as I already
know) that you are very nice, love your
children and are grateful to people . . .
Phone, please, Marina, when you return to
Dallas. I don't understand at all why you
have neither written nor phoned.

February 9: I can come by to pick you (and the children) up when it is convenient, and we can
spend a day here as we did in April. I am
not afraid of the newsmen. Let them ask:
"Well, what happened when you saw Mrs.
Oswald?"—"Oh, we talked about children
as usual."

"I have never understood [it] to this day," Ruth says of her
decades-long estrangement from Marina, though she now realizes how, within hours of the assassination, the Russian woman
had begun accumulating grievances with the imaginative energy
of her mother-in-law, Marguerite. A month after having told
the DCLU that Ruth remained a good friend, Marina would be
telling the Warren Commission this about Mrs. Paine:

She likes to be well known, popular, and I think that anything that I should write her, for example, would wind up in
the press.
    The reason that I think so is that the first time we were in
jail to see Lee, she was with me and with her children, and
she was trying to get in front of the cameras, and to push her

children and instructed her children to look this way and
look that way. And the first photographs that appeared were
of me and her children.

It is hard to lose the impression that Marina, now ready for her
close-up, has had it spoiled by Mrs. Paine.
Shown this testimony decades later, Ruth reacts with deliberate calm: "Wow. I've never read that. Let's start with the
facts. One child was there." She judges Marina "disappointingly
vulnerable to [the] influence of other people around her—understandable in *that* circumstance: new to the country and not
knowing who to believe or what to think, and being very scared
of being sent back. But still, it surprises me that she didn't think
of me as somebody she could trust. And she clearly didn't, but I
think mostly because of what other people said . . ."
    This was partially true; Marina was surrounded by a whole
new business and legal apparatus. Yet within ten days of the assassination her feelings toward Ruth had found an irrational
focus, not through some third party's influence, but from yet
another act of kindness by Ruth herself. On November 30, Ruth
had sent Marina, via the Irving police, along with letters and
baby clothes, her copy of КНИГА ПОЛЕЗНЫХ СОВЕТОВ, the thick
book of Russian housekeeping advice that Lee, so particular
about his shirts and potatoes, had given Marina for a twenty-
first birthday present. Ruth thought the item would make Marina, wherever she was, less homesick; she did not know that,
between the book's chartreuse covers, lay something more than
tips on first aid, knitting, and permanent waves. Hidden inside
was a series of instructions to Marina from Lee himself, the

document he had left for her on a desk back at the Neely Street apartment last April 10, just before he went out to shoot at General Walker.

The eleven numbered points of the note informed Marina that the rent and gas were paid up, told her where to find her husband's post office box, instructed her to send the Soviet embassy any press clippings that might result from this freelance bit of revolutionary action, and suggested how she get by in his absence:

9. We have *friends* here, and the *Red Cross* will also help you.
10. I left you as much money as I could . . . you and Junie can live for two months on $10 a week.
11. If I am alive and taken prisoner, the city jail is at the end of the bridge we always used to cross when we went to town. . . .

For seven months Marina had kept the list as something to hold over her husband's head, a kind of insurance policy against further bad behavior. Now its discovery by the Secret Service, who had inspected the book Ruth sent over, linked Lee, for the first time, to the Walker shooting. The authorities also, suddenly, saw new reason to be suspicious of Oswald's up-to-now cooperative widow—and, however illogically, Ruth herself. On Monday, December 2, two Secret Service men came out to Irving and exhibited the kind of excited hostility Ruth had not experienced since the Dallas police first showed up ten days before.

"One of them was their Russian-speaking person," she remembers. "He led off, in Russian"—perhaps a hostile gesture or an investigative trick—"and showed me this piece of paper, and said have I seen this; and I said no, and do I know who wrote it, and I said no . . . and he said, 'Well, Mrs. Paine, you sent this to Mrs. Oswald.' And I said no, no. And we went back and forth quite a bit. It was one of the worst moments, I would say, in the whole time for me. Because he was the first, and essentially has been the only [law-enforcement figure], to call me a liar."

Michael Paine remembers being in the kitchen when this confrontation took place: "I couldn't hear what they were saying, but I heard Ruth's tone of voice—scared, and being outrageously harassed." She herself recalls how the second Secret Service man finally "said that it was in a book. And I said, 'Well, I sent a book.' And meantime, all I saw of the note was that it referred to the key for the post office box." The single page the agent put in front of Ruth had no salutation or signature. Only later, when she saw an article in the *Houston Chronicle* that mentioned some of the note's elements, including the key, would she understand what had been shown to her.*

"If she'd wanted to help Marina," Michael Paine points out today, "she would have burned it." (Had Marina herself remem-

---

*Realizing that Marina had withheld this information did not deter Ruth in her quest to reestablish contact: She sought to understand the fear that might have motivated her friend. But she did go so far as to concede to Bardwell Odum, the FBI agent, that keeping the secret was "a moral failing" on Marina's part. Reminded of this judgment in the year 2000, a somewhat tougher Ruth exclaims: "Good for me!"

bered the note before the authorities found it, *she* undoubtedly would have, just as she had burned her copies of the backyard rifle photographs.) The Secret Service and FBI would eventually recover their logic on this point, but it is unclear how long it took Marina to do the same. She reacted to the incident in the manner of her late husband and mother-in-law, finding emotional convenience in irrationality. If she could blame Ruth for this new piece of trouble, then she needn't feel guilty over eating Ruth's food, or roiling Ruth's life, or abandoning Ruth herself. She needn't feel guilty about hiding her knowledge of the gun. This was the great psychological dividend paid by discovery of the "Walker letter," no matter what short-term difficulty it caused Marina with the authorities.

The contributions to Oswald's widow amounted eventually to around $70,000—several times that in today's money. She soon required a printed, black-bordered response card—*Thank you, Mrs. Marina N. Oswald and children*—to keep up with them. Before long she had a Fisher stereo, a charge card at Neiman-Marcus, a bouffant hairdo, and new dentistry through which to speak her rapidly improving English. In an essay written after release of the Warren Report, Elizabeth Hardwick would pronounce the assassin's widow "born for the American Southwest . . . as current as today's weather."

Three days after being confronted with the Walker letter, Marina dispatched Thorne and Martin and her brother-in-law to Irving to pick up whatever remained of her and Lee's possessions. Ruth and Michael helped load them into Robert Oswald's station wagon. Lee's brother, in Ruth's recollection, was not unpleasant on that day, but Robert hadn't dropped his suspicions of Michael Paine, whose own inquiries about Marina he found irritatingly "persistent."

Robert was seeing a lot of his sister-in-law these days. On long drives out to the cemetery where Lee was buried, he and Marina "might talk about almost any subject," he says, but on the way back the topic was always Lee. Marina convinced him that she had loved his brother, and in his 1967 book Robert more or less brushes off her knowledge of Lee's "earlier violent acts," including the Walker shooting. "I think she kept quiet about them because she hoped that Lee would gradually settle into a normal life." Before too long, Robert got Marina away from both Thorne and Martin, whom he regarded as opportunists, and moved her in with his own family in Denton, Texas. When Ruth drove out there in one more attempt to regain contact with Marina, Robert's wife, Vada, greeted her through the screen door but did not invite her inside or permit her to talk with anyone else.

Understanding that Robert was swept into the assassination disaster as accidentally as herself, Ruth has always forgiven his visceral dislike of her and Michael, which no doubt helped to shape Marina's more complicated estrangement: "Not knowing who we were," says Ruth, "the safe thing was to stay clear, and probably to advise her to stay clear." Certainly Marina's complaint about Ruth's supposed enjoyment of the limelight mimics Robert's own. But the influence of Lee's brother was stronger than Ruth ever knew. In the period after the assassination, Marina had a brief affair with Robert Oswald. Their involvement may have provided the chance for almost mythic mutual revenge against a brother and husband; surely it made the new gap be-

tween Marina and Ruth even less bridgeable. Marina was now
subject to both Robert's viewpoint and her own shame; the two
conditions conspired to lock out her old friend.[*]

In the late winter of '64, however, following her appearance
before the Warren Commission—and perhaps inspired by guilt
over her mean-spirited testimony concerning Ruth—Marina
finally proposed a meeting. "We met at Katya Ford's home, where
she was staying," Ruth recalls, "and that was comforting, to know
that she had remade contact with Russian-speaking folks." The
meeting was brief and friendly but not anything that could be
judged a success. No mention was made of the Walker letter or
other reasons for the breach. Marina's essential message seemed
to be that the Warren Commissioners "were nice people, and
they would be kind and thoughtful, that I shouldn't be worried
about going to testify."

Ruth felt distant and bewildered, and a final meeting that fall
didn't change things. By then Marina wanted to show off the new
house she'd bought north of Dallas. "We took a picture and we
talked for a little bit, and I saw her children, and she saw mine,
and so on. We caught up a little on child kinds of issues. But I

---

[*]Priscilla Johnson McMillan, whose *Marina and Lee* (1977) remains the most
authoritative and insightful study of the Oswalds' marriage, heard about the
affair from Marina herself but never mentioned it in her book a quarter century ago. She thinks highly of Robert Oswald, even if he would not cooperate
with her research. "He's gone on and led a decent life and tried to raise his
children with that name." But the affair (confirmed by this author's conversation with another source once close to Marina) is relevant to any understanding of Ruth Paine's position, and when Mrs. McMillan revealed it to me
in August 2000, it was with the thought that finally knowing about it "might
lighten Ruth's load a little bit."

found it . . . I was very sad." The two women have not been in touch for more than thirty-five years.*

None of the Oswalds—Lee, Marina, Marguerite, or Robert— had been much equipped by their own experience to understand a vessel of disinterested kindness like Ruth Paine. Lee's mother, who speculated that the assassination had been a government-sponsored "mercy-killing," and who thought her son, like JFK, deserved burial in Arlington, pronounced Ruth a "strange woman" not long after the day in 1964 when she showed up at 2515 West Fifth asking to take pictures "for the historical record." Ruth obliged, even if Marguerite "was not friendly, I would say." The elder Mrs. Oswald departed the house within minutes. Among the milder annotations in her copy of the Warren Commission transcripts, preserved at Texas Christian University with a ragbag of her other papers, is the comment "This woman is a liar" beside Ruth Paine's testimony. Even Ruth, so devoid of mockery, now has trouble taking Marguerite Oswald, who died in 1981, with complete seriousness: "She was a trip."

---

*As early as 1965, when beginning work on her book (with Marina Oswald's close cooperation), Mrs. McMillan wrote to Ruth about Marina's "low self-esteem" and general instability, as well as the guilt the young woman felt "to an almost crippling extent" over her debt to Ruth. Today, she says: "Ruth was good to her . . . and Marina thinks she's so evil that it's more than she can stand, to be on the receiving [end] and to face up to what she did to Ruth's life."

Mrs. McMillan still sees Marina as a mercurial combination of self-loathing and self-regard. "Marina was very quick to impute sexual interest in her to everybody," Mrs. McMillan told me in August 2000. Apprehension of a sexual interest on Ruth's part may have clouded matters between the two women even before the assassination. Mrs. McMillan had hoped that Marina would eventually seek a full reconciliation with the woman who had helped

Robert is a harder figure to reckon with. A dignified and in many ways admirable man, he rarely does interviews, and never on the telephone. He cannot be coaxed to sit down for a face-to-face discussion of the Paines. "No, sir, not on this issue," he says politely. Asked if he would at least like to disavow the suspicions he long ago raised against Ruth and Michael in his book about Lee, he declines the opportunity: "I will not comment on it."

Nor will Marina respond to a request for her present-day thoughts about Ruth. "I read your letter," she tells me over the telephone, her voice still overlaid with its Russian accent and an unmistakable frost. "I'm not interested." She did speak with Oprah Winfrey to help advance a conspiracy theory of the assassination on its thirty-third anniversary in 1996. By then the modern glamor girl perceived by Elizabeth Hardwick had long since disappeared, along with the money. Her face lined, her whole manner careworn, Marina seemed more a Soviet relic than a faded American success. She was still living in Texas, working in a retail store.

Watching a videotape of the *Oprah* interview in the late spring of 2000, Ruth gets her first look at the older Marina. She watches with attention and composure, murmuring recognition when her former friend mentions the surge of embarrassment she had to feel over eating the bread of her "Quaker friend"

---

her so much; she judges it "unconscionable" that, after four decades, Marina still hasn't. Marina Oswald Porter's latter-day embrace of conspiracy theories may have something to do with a need, even now, to rescue her sense of self-worth. "For history's sake," says Mrs. McMillan, "it would be a good thing if Marina had been as good a person as Ruth."

while keeping secret the location and history of her husband's gun. After the VCR shuts off, Ruth quietly concedes the impossibility of ever having maintained a friendship with the young woman who provided exotic solace in the lonely year of 1963. "What did we share," she asks, her eyes filling with tears, "but the worst thing that had happened to either of us?"

Part Three  History

# One

R uth Paine gave her first testimony in the matter of John F. Kennedy's assassination on December 5, 1963, in Irving, to Mr. Dirk Kunert of the Senate Subcommittee on Internal Security. Soon abandoned for the Warren Commission's more wide-ranging investigation, the SIS probe has long been forgotten by almost everyone, including Ruth. But the transcript made on December 5 shows her exceptionally eager to cooperate, as she pronounces the FBI agents she's been seeing "remarkable people." Indeed, she's "never felt so pleased about paying [her] taxes."

The Oswald family found such effusiveness distasteful and suspicious, but most people who have spent a single, relaxed hour in Ruth Paine's company will not regard this kind of utterance as ingenuous or effortful, and anyone familiar with what the Dallas police put her through on November 22 will recognize the particular remark quoted above as a sigh of relief over her deliverance to another jurisdiction.

By early December the FBI was conducting what one internal memo described as the bureau's own "full scale intelligence type investigation" to develop "detailed information on both RUTH and MICHAEL PAINE as to education, employment, relatives, associates, travel, and financial activity." The Paines' existence would soon be almost as minutely accounted for as Lee

Oswald's own—in some ways more so, given the more stable patterns and traceable connections in their lives. The FBI collected more data than most scholarly biographers, though most of it would be left raw—cubic feet of information it was less important to organize than to screen for any anomalies and inexplicables. Perhaps most pertinent to the examiners was the simple assertion, by multiple sources, that any assistance offered by Ruth to Marina Oswald was entirely consistent with Mrs. Paine's character—i.e., that it did not need to be explained as a conspiracy's maintenance of the assassin's wife.

Family and friends; acquaintances from Ohio, Philadelphia, Irving, and every point in Ruth's summer travels; ministers and mentors; neighbors; family doctors and former roommates—all were interviewed. Each one's comments, paraphrased on Form FD-302, joined an immense chorus assuring investigators that Mrs. Paine was "kind, intelligent, conscientious," "dedicated to doing good for humanity," "a charming, intelligent person and a completely loyal American citizen," "genuinely interested in the misfortunes of other people," "a sincere Christian," "of high moral character, above-average intelligence," and "the most dedicated Quaker [the interviewee] had ever met." The only person who could blush from reading anything in the FBI's compilation—vastly too voluminous to be called a "file"—is Ruth herself.*

---

*When shown some of this material four decades later, Ruth dissents from one description of herself as a "flighty-type individual." But her often fizzy manner is a fact of her life, a kind of runoff generated by pleasure in the world and secure faith in God. The gaiety—not without its shy, nervous aspect—is more reflective of moral seriousness than at odds with it. Ruth does not dis-

Bank statements, address books, phone bills, personal letters: the Paines' ordinary paper trail supplemented the massive
oral history to detail a picture of the couple's values, personal
relations, and politics. The long-ago affiliations of Ruth's and
Michael's parents got scrutinized with the more recent operations of the East-West Contacts Committee and Young Friends
pen-pal program. Even Bill and Carol Hyde's involvement in
the consumer cooperative movement, a quarter-century before
in New York City, attracted the investigators' notice. Mrs. Hyde
told two FBI agents that, as a little girl, Ruth had absorbed a particular sort of anti-Communism, because her parents

> had many run-ins with the Communists who were active in
> [their cooperative] group. [Mrs. Hyde] said that she and her
> former husband were very much aware of how the Commu-
> nists would operate in this type of organization in order to
> get their opinions over to other individuals in the group,
> and they had often discussed these tactics when her daugh-
> ter was present.

Ruth, who was taken to a Norman Thomas rally at the age of
eight, can recall those conversations even today ("They *hated*
the Communists—oh, boy!"), but her own aversion to Commu-
nism came in part from the Quaker beliefs she acquired independent of her parents. She would explain to the Warren

---

pute Priscilla McMillan's characterization of her, in *Marina and Lee*, as "a
little bit fey," but admits, with an embarrassed smile, that she had to look up
the word when she read it in Mrs. McMillan's book.

Commission that her pacifism, however nonabsolute, could not
accommodate Marxism: "No; they don't go together . . . You
can't believe violent overthrow and be a pacifist."

The FBI had taken control of Ruth's personal papers (those
metal file boxes) from the Dallas police on January 15, 1964.
Probably the most painful of those documents were the letters to
Dr. Harding, written in 1960, during her mother's commitment
to the sanitarium. The difficult family dynamic they addressed
may not have had any evidentiary value to an investigation of the
President's murder, but some of Ruth's assertions, particularly
about how she would try "to report only what has happened to
me personally," and has attempted to consider whether it is
"right to speak intimately of other people without their knowledge or consent," gave a preview of how the Warren Commission's principal witness (Ruth Paine's testimony occupies more
pages than anyone else's) would also be the most precise and
morally interesting person to come before it.


Ruth prepared for her appearance before the Commission by
translating, from Russian back into English, the drafts of her
letters to Marina. Then, in mid-March of '64, she traveled to
Washington with Michael and her mother. Checked into a "very
nice elderly hotel" with a view of the Washington Monument,
she stayed up late the night before her testimony was to begin,
trying to get ready. "I got a cold, in fact, and had to get an antibi-
otic shot in the rear to keep going. I wanted to lay out what I did
know that could be in any way useful; and to consider then that I

had *done* what I needed to do for history. So I wanted it to be as complete as I could make it, and as accurate."

The Commission staff had already fed itself on hundreds of FBI and police interviews, material that raised just a handful of red flags about Ruth's own conduct: Counsel David Belin wanted to know if she really had said "we were expecting you" to the police, and there was a curious notation on the March 1963 page of her Hallmark pocket calendar that needed, to say the least, clarification: "★—LHO purchase of rifle."

The explanation of the latter was fairly simple. Ruth had made this post-facto jotting when the story of Oswald's mailorder gun-buying came out in news reports. "I was trying to figure out where it fit into things," she explains today—trying to reconstruct, in future Watergate parlance, what she hadn't known and when she hadn't known it. "I was also really spaced out at that point. I wasn't functioning too well."*

But by March, even with a cold and through the scrim of her sometimes confusing charm, Ruth Paine was ready to offer history a clearly observed texture of the Oswalds' marriage and movements in the months and hours prior to President Kennedy's murder. Those who disbelieve the Warren Report's conclusions have often dismissed Ruth as the Commission's darling, though they would no doubt have found sullenness and imprecision just as suspicious in their assaults on the findings.

---

*The idea that she would have made a written notation of the purchase at the time it occurred—as if she were the recording secretary of a conspiracy—defies logic as much as the theory that she deliberately "sent" Marina the Walker letter inside the household-hints book in December.

Ruth remembers Chief Justice Earl Warren as "courteous" and "welcoming," though he declined to ask many questions himself; Congressman Ford was similarly quiet. Along with considerable evidence of the witness's character, the transcript of Ruth's testimony reveals bits of the various Commission members' personalities: Hale Boggs, for example, the Louisiana congressman, self-importantly rushes through some questions already covered during his absence the day before so that he can get to "a meeting at the Speaker's office." Georgia's Sen. Richard Russell, filibustering the civil-rights bill that week, was the only Commissioner Ruth never saw.

Senior Counsel Albert E. Jenner, Jr., the distinguished Chicago attorney in charge of Oswald's background and motivation would conduct Ruth's deposition and ask most of the questions put to her in the full session.* The two of them shared an appreciation of exact language (he commented on a split infinitive in the draft of her *Look* article), and she was not at all bothered by his strict policing of the border between simple recollection and inference—or what he called "rationalization." The transcript of Ruth's first afternoon of testimony runs to forty-five pages of closely spaced, small-point type. It gives an impression of rather chilly relations between the main questioner and witness, but Ruth remembers nothing like hostility. She does, however, recall the Commissioners growing more comfortable as time went on, with Jenner increasingly willing "to let me narrate, rather than [answer] one question after another."

---

*Jenner (1907–88) later served as minority counsel to the House Judiciary Committee during its impeachment proceedings against President Nixon.

In accordance with Quaker practice, Ruth elected to "affirm" rather than swear to the truth of her testimony,* but when it's pointed out to her, years later, that she ran *counter* to Friends custom in addressing Jenner as "sir," she laughs, pronouncing the deviation only "a sign of having taken in Texas. I didn't use 'sir' at all until I'd been there a little while."

The testimony, which generated another 183 pages of transcript in the two days that followed, reads like a cross between drawing-room drama and memory play. A range of in-the-moment moods jibes with, and cuts against, the year-old events being recollected. At this long remove, the dialogue sometimes startles with antique touches (Marina and Ruth are referred to as "you girls"), but its creepy moments remain timelessly potent:

> MR. JENNER:  For the record, I am placing the rifle in the folded blanket as Mrs. Paine folded it. This is being done without the rifle being dismantled.
>
> May the record show, Mr. Chairman, that the rifle fits well in the package from end to end, and it does not—
>
> MRS. PAINE:  Can you make it flatter?
>
> MR. JENNER:  No; because the rifle is now in there.
>
> MRS. PAINE:  I just mean that—
>
> MR. JENNER:  Was that about the appearance of the blanket wrapped package that you saw on your garage floor?
>
> MRS. PAINE:  Yes; although I recall it as quite flat.

---

*From Quakerism's earliest days, "the implication of oath taking was to the effect that when not under oath there was no special necessity to abide by the truth." (Charles M. Woodman, *Quakers Find a Way*, 1950.)

Perhaps the most poignant exchange involved a point of semantics:

MR. JENNER: This was the weekend [November 9] he was home?

MRS. PAINE: This was the weekend that he was home, which was the last weekend he was home, don't call it home though.

MR. JENNER: I am sorry.

At times one can see the Commissioners beginning to glaze over. Even Jenner, with such masses of material to consider, could lose sight of basic circumstances. During a cab ride together, he surprised Ruth by seeming not to know "that Michael's family had money . . . that was so fundamental."

The investigators' very thoroughness assured some black-comic incidents. During the same week that Ruth testified in Washington, the FBI contacted Mr. William Esslinger in Atlanta, asking to know why he appeared in Mrs. Paine's address book. Mr. Esslinger admitted to living in Dallas between May 1960 and June 1963, but knew no one "by the name of PAINE" there and "had no idea why his name, address, and telephone in Dallas should be of any interest to any person" so named. Mr. Esslinger proceeded to call his wife, but when he did, she too couldn't figure out the matter.

One imagines Mr. Esslinger starting to sweat, a Josef K. moment beginning to build in the middle of an ordinary day, as he finds himself being connected to the crime of the century. Relief comes only when—*yes!*—he can recall "very vaguely that sometime during the late fall of 1962, he obtained a partially grown cat for his daughter from a family in Irving, Texas. He believed the family having this cat may possibly have lived on Fifth Street in Irving. He said Fifth Street came to his mind because he recalled having experienced difficulty in locating the residence of this family."

*Of course!* It all came back now, and went into the report:

> a young girl in the family from which he obtained the cat suffered from an allergy which prevented her from keeping the cat. This girl was greatly attached to the cat and her mother at the time made a note of ESSLINGER's name and telephone number in the event the girl desired to inquire about the cat at a later date.

There was no need to confirm this explanation with Lynn Paine's pediatric allergist. Dr. Salmon Halpern, on the "H" page of Ruth's address book, had already had his FBI interview, and he told Agent Raymond J. Fox that "Mrs. RUTH PAINE has visited his office on several occasions with her small child who has an allergy." Dr. Halpern "never discussed MARINA OSWALD with her."

If the story of Mr. Esslinger carries a certain nightmarish charm, it also acts as a miniature allegory. His implication in the events—accidental, temporary, tangential—is, in its way, an inconsequential version of Ruth's own, which depended on the collision of innocent intentions and unforeseen enormities.

On Monday, March 23, three days after concluding her testi-

mony before the full Commission, Ruth Paine welcomed Albert
Jenner to 2515 West Fifth Street in Irving to have a look at her
house. Another great stretch of deposition generated as the
senior counsel and an FBI man measured various objects and
rooms.

Jenner had Ruth step into the garage and turn on the light.
The interior, if minus the rifle, was otherwise just as cluttered
as it had been four months ago. "He did find the garage a bit of a
mess," Ruth now recalls. "Definitely a tidy guy, Jenner." The
blocks that she had lacquered on the night before the killing
were still there and, for some reason, in need of measuring:

MR. JENNER: John Joe, will you measure that which Mrs.
Paine describes as a block and which I describe as a box?
AGENT HOWLETT: It is $\frac{1}{4}''$ wide by $2'$ long.
MR. JENNER: How deep?
AGENT HOWLETT: It is $7\frac{1}{2}''$ deep, with $\frac{1}{2}''$ press plywood
on the bottom, makes it a total heighth of $8''$.

Jenner, narrating his movement from room to room like the
voice behind the video camera he would be using today, notes
that the front "lawn area is entirely open except for the oak
tree"—whose circumference he promises to measure in a moment. The eminent lawyer sounds, at moments, more like a
contractor.

The government investigators had, at this point, the same
faith in minutiae that conspiracy theorists would display in the
decades to come. The Commissioners sought to shake out every
millimeter of space and half-second of time in order to say: see,

nothing lurks here. The dissenters even now believe that the same parcels, shaken harder and sifted more finely, will give up the glinting husk of the conspiracy's seed. "Facts" have been, as in Mr. Gradgrind's school, "the one thing needful" to both sides, but the ghost of Oswald, perhaps still playing with Junie under the oak tree, has always been beyond the reach of anyone's tape measure.

Ruth did get the impression, during Jenner's Irving visit, "that they were going into *extraordinary* detail," but she "didn't mind them overdoing it." She shared the belief that exhaustiveness would, in fact, exhaust the matter—the questions and the doubts, if not the grief—and she showed a meticulousness of her own, paying $154.65 for a court-reporter's transcript of her testimony and sending the Commission careful emendations to the Irving deposition. It was easy to correct the spelling of Linnie Mae Randle's name, but it required sharp attention to restore a crucial, missing pronoun:

MRS. PAINE: Yes—I translated the question, asking Marina if she knew if Lee had a rifle, and she said, "Yes,"— she had seen sometime previously—seen a rifle which she knew to be in this roll . . .

Pg. 49. Word omitted *Line 20.* "seen a rifle which she knew to be *his* in this roll. . . ."

In front of the full Commission, Ruth had mentioned her distress over being asked to give "details on things I don't recall that well." But she was conversely determined to supply every morsel she actually had. Today she tells the story of what happened when she announced to the members that she wanted to give them a piece of information she had previously withheld (out of embarrassment): "And they all leaned forward like 'this is going to be exciting' "—only to hear her admit that, prior to giving the permitless Lee Oswald his driving lesson in an empty parking lot (legal), she had allowed him to drive the car from 2515 West Fifth to the lot (illegal).

Upon release of the Warren Report in October 1964, Ruth wrote the Commission to convey admiration for "the scope of your investigation and the dedication and sheer energy brought to it by yourselves and your staff." But in another letter, written the same week and addressed solely to Wesley J. Liebeler, the Commission lawyer most concerned with Oswald's motivation, she admitted anxiety over whether the formal circumstances in which testimony had been taken allowed for the fullest expression of essentials:

> Somehow truth about another person's character and inner feelings is better sought in an atmosphere where one can be vulnerable, and feel a mistaken perception has time and opportunity to be found and corrected. The search requires opportunity to stumble over half-formed thoughts, vaguely recalled impressions, and one's own personal biases and failings.

In an age of ever-growing relativism, Ruth Paine, a woman whose interests embraced astrology, felt impelled to part any veils obscuring the *literal* truth of what had transpired on and before November 22. Amidst her personal papers is the draft of her letter to Liebeler; it includes the following paragraph, crossed out and never sent, but more interesting than all the rest:

> I've been seeing a psychiatrist in Dallas for the purpose of giving attention to my sundry problems—one of them being a wish to distinguish accurately between what I think and what the facts warrant thinking. He gives me no satisfaction in this pursuit at all, saying everyone brings the bias of his own background to the events he participates in or observes. My mother has said we can only be as honest as our insight permits us. It's true, but I still pursue honesty as an end in itself.

Ruth Paine may be one of the few Americans of her time to have seen a psychiatrist in the hope of being told she was wrong about something instead of right, in an effort to place truth above feelings. The years have made these aborted utterances to Liebeler even more remarkable—nearly unintelligible to an age whose celebration of subjectivity infects the composition of everything from history to plea bargains.

The degree to which *she* may have affected *events*, rather than the other way around, remained uppermost in Ruth's mind throughout 1964. To the Warren Commission she offers very little in the way of confession or self-exculpation, but when she makes remarks that can be categorized as such, they almost always concern the question of whether or not her attentions to Marina had emasculated Lee—with whatever dire consequences. A conversation she had with Penelope Rainey, a Philadelphia friend, during her summer trip in '63, seems especially to have troubled her memory:

> I recall one important thing in what I said to Mrs. Rainey, that I never said in conversation to anyone else, that I was worried about offending Lee, that if offended, or if he felt I was taking his wife or not doing what he wanted in the situation, that he might be angry with me, and that I didn't want to subject myself or my children to possible harm from him.
>
> She is the only person to whom I mentioned my thought that he might possibly be a person who could cause harm, and there was a very, not a strong thought in my thinking at all, but should be registered as having at least occurred to me, that he could be angry to the point of violence in relation to me.

In her October 1964 letter to the Commission, Ruth acknowledges that Oswald "must have had severely mixed feelings about [Marina's] being at my home," but she still wants it known that she put "the invitation in a context which did not compete with or belittle Oswald's ability to care for Marina himself." Marina *herself* may not have been "as careful about his feelings in this regard."

Even so, as time went on, others would continue to blame Ruth for undermining Lee's manhood and self-esteem. Robert Oswald declares in his book that "the friendship between Ruth Paine and Marina," once begun in February 1963, "apparently contributes to Lee's feeling of rejection and failure"—a notion he may have sold to his sister-in-law. Ruth herself would make a point of saving one addled piece of mail, a kind of sympathetic hate letter, from a woman in Los Angeles: "Lee could have had the hope, to save him. You even took Marina, for Your purposes, you caused Marina to reject him, his last chance at manhood, when he was clutching then the very last straw!"

No one, of course, can outdo Marguerite Oswald on the matter. Her handwriting shrieks up and down the margins of Ruth's testimony about her son's marriage:

> The proud and perfect Quaker . . . I keep saying she is a fraud and liar . . . I can hardly read this woman's thoughts. She is evil, and selfish and the cause of it all. You ought to be horse-whipped.

When Ruth admits having worried that Oswald might turn physically against her, Marguerite seems to cheer her son on toward more, posthumous violence: "I would wipe up the floor with her."*

It is hardly a surprise to find Marguerite flinging the word "evil" in Ruth's direction; one suspects that Mrs. Paine's closer resemblance to the quality's opposite frightened the assassin's mother to some degree. But the "banality of evil" was much in the air when the Warren Commission held its hearings. Hannah

---

*Marguerite's resentment of Ruth is further inflamed by her entirely predictable sense that the Commission didn't show her the same courtesy Mrs. Paine received. "I had to beg for a break," she writes on page 41 of Volume III, beside John McCloy's suggestion that the Commission take "a little recess" from Ruth's testimony.

Arendt's *Eichmann in Jerusalem*, which carried the phrase in its subtitle, could be found in almost any bookstore, and Ruth's most analytical testimony about Oswald, quoted below, seems to echo Arendt's thinking on Eichmann:

> It seems to me important, very important, to the record that we face the fact that this man was not only human but a rather ordinary one in many respects, and who appeared ordinary.
>
> If we think that this was a man such as we might never meet, a great aberration from the normal, someone who would stand out in a crowd as unusual, then we don't know this man, we have no means of recognizing such a person again in advance of a crime such as he committed.

Ruth also tries to underline Oswald's ordinary *goodness*— his affection for his daughters, his occasional helpfulness on the weekends. Her October letter to the Commission disputes the Warren Report's assertion that Lee was lying in 1961 when he wrote the American Embassy in Moscow about Marina's having been hospitalized for "nervous exhaustion." The Commission based its conclusion on a denial from his wife, but Ruth remembered Marina once mentioning to her "a time she was hospitalized when pregnant with June." So, possibly, "when Marina was asked whether she had been hospitalized for 'nervous exhaustion' the Russian sentence put to her implied (as does the English) hospitalized for a mental disorder."

Why bother straightening out this especially minor point?

Only for the sake of honesty ("an end in itself") and, in some in-
finitesimal measure, as a favor to Oswald's hideously encum-
bered soul.

The Commission's charge was to find out what had happened
and, if at all possible, why. What-might-have-beens, except as
they related to possible reform of presidential-protection rules,
were left to ordinary citizens who lay awake at night, replaying
the assassination in their minds, and especially to the people
whose lives it had capsized. "I didn't know he had a gun," Ruth
wrote the New York *Journal-American*'s Guy Richards in December of '63, "and shall forever have to live with my regrets that
I did not perceive this incompetent yet striving man as a dangerous person." Throughout her testimony, depositions, interviews, and correspondence, Ruth comes across as a woman
more naturally forward-looking than retrospective, but she
cannot resist fingering several small pieces of fate that have
already, irreversibly, played themselves out.

Two of them in particular: What if she had given Jim Hosty
Lee's rooming-house phone number during one of the agent's
early-November visits? He could then have used a reverse
directory to get the address she didn't know; a closer FBI tab
on Oswald, or a confrontation, might somehow have thwarted
the imminent meeting of motive and opportunity. And there
was the November 10 embassy letter: What if she had pressed
Michael harder to read it, and what if it had spurred either one
of them to action?

She pondered small ineffables ("Suppose I had not had a
birthday party the weekend before the assassination and Marina

had not told Lee to stay away? I am left with the speculation whether this tiny matter might have made a difference"); and she faced the blunt questions posed by others: "While you were taking care of Mrs. Oswald, didn't this give Oswald more money to buy guns?"

One can riddle things further and further back—suppose Ruth had not, in the 1950s, felt God calling her to study a foreign language? And what if, in heeding the call, she had picked Chinese instead of Russian? But then, and now, the mystery lay within Lee, not Ruth. She has always found it odd that he would leave the garage light on—as odd as his leaving the embassy letter out on her desk. Did he, in the supposed manner of the ambivalent criminal, "want to be caught" before he acted? Was he trying to provoke suspicions, questions?* Ruth, finally, doesn't think so: she continues to see these acts more as evidence of a growing distraction, a falling apart—in their small way, more predictive than preventive of what Oswald would do in Dealey Plaza.

But when Lee asked Marina to take an apartment with him the following day, was he hoping the nonlethal part of his personality might overrule his murderous intentions for Friday? It's possible, Ruth now says, and yet, "if he really wanted to be talked out of a self-destruct course, he didn't know how to do it, how to get her assistance in it . . . It's the urgency she couldn't respond to, it seems to me. To do it right away." And even if Ma-

---

*Marguerite's marginalia insists that someone else left the light on: Lee "*always* turned off lights. Ecomy [*sic*] reasons."

rina had somehow said yes: Does Ruth believe *that* would have short-circuited the plan to kill Kennedy? "I don't," she says.

Asked, more generally, whether she expected what we would now call "closure" from the Warren Report, Ruth answers, "I expected more than was achieved"—which is putting it mildly. For those disinclined to believe the assassination could have been committed by a "lone nut," the Report was a giant false bridge from crime to conclusion that they refused to cross. But it was a wonderful span nonetheless, available for disassembly into a million girders and rivets, all of which could be jerry-rigged into a new bridge leading somewhere else entirely.

Even a reader convinced of all the Report's basic conclusions, including the single-bullet theory, can now find, lurking within the twenty-six volumes of testimony and exhibits, one might-have-been more shimmering than the rest. When asked by the Commission to give what she thought Michael's first impression of the Oswalds had been on April 2, 1963, Ruth answers: "he didn't give me this impression as at the time we didn't talk that much . . . not living together we talked together very little. I am sure he would have given me his impression if we had been having dinner together the next day afterwards, you see."

Along with this impression, one piece of information that might have been imparted the following night, while passing the peas—*By the way . . .*—never got offered. It truly might have made all the difference, but Ruth would not have it for another thirty years.

# Two

The Kennedy assassination is still regularly presented—to those Americans who remember it and to the large majority who don't—as a milestone of modernity, the weekend that television news, however gruesomely, "came into its own." But to anyone reconstructing the event's aftermath, the months following November 1963 now seem a low-tech, slow-moving affair, almost sepia-tinted.

When Mrs. Hyde writes her daughter on December 3, she types up, rather than Xeroxes, an AP article she's found at the Oberlin College library. In another letter, she urges Ruth to telephone "if there should be occasion to do so." But FBI records show that, between November 22 and December 18, the Paines allowed themselves to make only fourteen long-distance calls from BLackburn 3-1628—not because they feared the wiretap no doubt on the line, but because, no matter how odd one's current circumstances, even fifteen toll calls was a lot in those pricey, pre-deregulated days.

The Dallas police department had not yet acquired a tape recorder to preserve anything said, in the last forty-eight hours of his life, by the most notorious suspect it would ever hold. When the Warren Commission decided, during his testimony, that it needed Michael to provide a sample of the packing tape Oswald had available to him at the Paines' home, he was told he could just mail it once he got back to Texas. A letter from Ruth to the Commission justified an 8¢ airmail stamp, the fastest means available. Some of the witnesses' depositions—bearing TOP SECRET rubber stampings that now look like comic epaulets atop each page—were run off in purple ditto-machine ink. There is even a Cold War antiquity to Ruth's Hallmark datebook, which, along with a chart showing the appropriate gift for each wedding anniversary, presents a guide for interpreting siren alerts in the National Civil Defense Code.

The blankness of that calendar's December pages bespeaks no sudden leisure in the owner's life, but rather something like the opposite. During the last weeks of 1963, as the datebook remained in the hands of investigators, Ruth was trying not only to locate Marina and take care of her own family, but also to deal with the continuing interest of the world press. "For Ruth Paine it was a new and exciting existence," Jim Bishop would write in *The Day Kennedy Was Shot* (1968). "Within the span of one afternoon, she had been whirled up and out of the drab life of dirty diapers and high chairs and the Book-of-the-Month Club and set onto the edges of the story of the century. She was a celebrity. Policemen, reporters, and photographers hung on her words . . . To a woman hitherto stranded on the sandbars of marital discord, this was an exciting ride down the rapids." Today, Ruth responds evenly to this overwritten bit of sarcasm: "He makes it sound like I'm having a good time. Less bored I was, but very sad, through all of that period."

She mostly fought to contain, not capitalize on, the excitement. The closest she had to a modern media advisor was David Forbes—Michael's uncle, and a lawyer with the family firm in Boston—whom she called in December. As Mr. Forbes would

tell the FBI: "she was being badgered by newspaper and magazine people regarding her association with MARINA and LEE
HARVEY OSWALD." His advice was simplicity itself—"to report the
facts accurately and to cooperate with these people or they
would continue to badger her"—and Ruth went on to follow it.
Her mother-in-law warned that the press were "almost as un-
predictable as a mob (or a wild animal at times)," but Ruth remembers how she soon found her footing with the reporters: "I
quickly learned that a few of them were not as well prepared or
as good as others—I got pretty discriminating about newsmen—
but it was interesting to talk to them."

She cooperated steadily—not in the overexcited manner of
that first night in the police station, but with patience and pre-
cision, taking their phone calls, composing answers to their
queries on the same typewriter that had rolled out her Antioch
papers and Oswald's embassy letter. Among the most important
visitors was William Manchester, who stayed up past midnight
with the Paines on September 20, 1964.* But Ruth spent time on
obscure freelancers, too, trying to make them comfortable with
*her*, offering reassurances that resembled the ones she had for-
merly tried conveying to Marina: She was getting as much, she
told them, as she gave. A few days after seeing Manchester, she
sent a letter to Helen Yenne, who had written pieces on Oswald's
psychology for the New York *Herald-Tribune* and the *Daily Texan*:

---

*In a footnote to *The Death of a President*, Manchester remarked that "Everyone who has questioned Ruth Paine, this writer included, has been impressed by her exceptional forthrightness."

It's hard to annoy me, and an irritation isn't apt to linger with me. So don't worry in any way about what or how you talk or write to me. I need no special handling.

You sense about me something few people have realized: that I have a need to talk about the assassination and the ensuing events. My personal world was deeply shaken, and my grief is still seeking a way to find its release. Somehow talking about it is a therapy I need.

There also remained the need, at least in her mother-in-law's eyes, for someone to write an article focusing on Ruth herself, one that would put her relation to events in a less limelit fashion than early reports had. Ruth recalls how Mrs. Young, "very aware of Cold War issues," was, in addition to much else, "worried about Lyman" and the hostility that might be directed at her ex-husband, an old leftist being connected to the assassination, if only at two removes. She thought any piece in *Look* would come too soon and be too poorly written "to help anyone but Marina Oswald," but an article done in a few months' time for another publication might yet serve to place her daughter-in-law's family in the proper perspective.

So Mrs. Young contacted the editor Norman Cousins, whom she knew from the World Federalist movement, to see what he could do; and on February 10, at her mother-in-law's urging, Ruth reluctantly wrote to the editor: "My own opinion is that nothing is needed in the way of public clarification, yet on the other hand, there would be no harm in having an article printed." Cousins may have come up with the idea of a piece to be written by Jessamyn West, the Quaker novelist well known for *The Friendly Persuasion.* Instead of his own *Saturday Review,* he suggested *Redbook,* where she could count on "sensitive" treatment.

Even with the condition that Cousins approve her text, West seemed enthusiastic about the assignment. From her home in Napa, California, she wrote Ruth: "As a lazy Quaker and semi-recluse, I rejoiced, from the moment I read of the help you had given the Oswalds, in *your* actions, as though they were a kind of substitute for my lack of action . . . I like many others I am sure was heartened amidst the horrors of November to read of someone whose concern it had been to keep, foster and conserve rather than to destroy."

Along with *The Friendly Persuasion,* Jessamyn West was known for being the cousin of Richard Nixon. "She was more my kind of Quaker than he," Ruth says today, with a laugh. The two women got on well when West came to Texas for several days in late February, shortly before Ruth's testimony to the Warren Commission. But the subject soon found herself not altogether happy with the writer's first draft. Ruth blushed—as she would have over those FBI reports—at the degree of sweet beneficence attributed to her. She didn't like coming off as a "naive do-gooder," but on March 28, in reply to this objection, West tried to get Ruth to take the characterization as a compliment:

Face it: "Do-gooder" is the term dreamed up by those too selfish and lethargic *to* do good, to justify their own unwillingness to make any effort for others. Martha may have been a "do gooder" but I have always been aware that Jesus, who could have had a fine spiritual talk with Mary under any tree, chose to go to the home, where somebody was busy in the kitchen . . . And face naive: it is the characteristic, in its good sense, of every artist and creator in the world: "a genuine innocent simplicity or lack of artificiality."

West's correspondence with Ruth, now in the Friends Library at Swarthmore College, is in some ways more interesting than the published article that prompted it. The letters make one consider how goodness is not only rare, but also unsettling. The truth is we are less likely to think about it than to "wrestle" with evil, as we claim to do all the time, in literature and on the op-ed page and on the split-screens of cable TV. We are less troubled by one person's malevolence than by another's kindness. To feel oneself less bad than somebody else is a relief, a pleasure to prolong; to judge oneself less good is an upsetting experience, a realization one prefers bringing to a quick close.

The ability of the unusually good person to perceive himself as such is ironically limited by humility, one of goodness's attendants. Only a few months after John Kennedy's assassination, three dozen New Yorkers witnessed the murder of Kitty Genovese from the safety of their apartments without so much as picking up the phone to call the police. Jessamyn West sent Ruth a clipping about the case, part of the effort to make her face, without embarrassment, the goodness within herself:

had you been one of these 37 persons, you would not, with worldly wisdom and a revulsion against do-goodism, have said to yourself, "She's probably drunk. She probably asked for it. It's none of my business. She may have a criminal record. I have my own family to think of." Etc. etc. I think you would have called the police then been out in the street, doing good.

One has no doubt about it. But the goodness that would assure a selfless response to any evil unfolding before Ruth's eyes may have handicapped her, beyond the average person, for recognizing the evil wrapped in a sullen, enigmatic personality such as Lee Harvey Oswald.

However she toned down her admiration, Jessamyn West remained, as the finished piece shows, enchanted by her subject:

> What she had done stuck in my mind more even than what Oswald or Ruby had done . . . when I met a tall girl, five-feet nine or ten, with a long brown bob, looking more like the campus than the kitchen and built more like a dancer than a Quaker (whatever that may mean, except that her outlines were more rakish than restrained), I was unable for the first hour to accept her as Ruth Paine. I talked with her as if she were someone empowered to speak for Ruth Paine.

West acknowledges to the reader that, after a week of interviewing, Ruth seemed "a much more worn and depressed person." The article's chief surprise comes with the subject's own admission that she was "glad" to hear of Ruby's killing Oswald, a sentiment that even with qualification ("this way would be so much easier for Marina'") rather shocks the author.

The piece ran in the July '64 issue of *Redbook*, and would stand as the first and last national publication to concern Ruth Paine herself. Ruth felt pleased enough by the final version to thank Barbara Lawrence, at the magazine, for sending a copy to Albert Jenner and

> for having the stack of copies sent me from the Dayton of-
> fice. I have given most of them to various friends and neigh-
> bors and it was helpful to be able to explain that these copies
> were sent to me by the publisher. (Somehow it is less em-
> barrassing that way, and people are pleased to accept the
> copy. But they would have felt funny about it if they thought I
> was putting out the 35¢ . . .)

Which is to say she would have felt self-aggrandizing.*

Ruth Paine donated her $500 *Redbook* fee to the American Civil Liberties Union.

Michael's reappearance in Ruth's life stood apart from all the assassination's other effects. In this one matter, the newsreel ran backward, restoring a piece of life instead of exploding it. At

---

*The previous December, *Look*'s T. George Harris had warned Ruth that "if the movie people ever understand your story you'll have trouble preventing them from a 'Desperate Hours' kind of fiction." One can't help feeling that today his equivalent would be alerting Ruth's to whatever methods would as-sure such an outcome, just as Marina would be weighing an offer, not only to talk to *Stern*, but to pose for *Playboy* as well.

first, Ruth had mixed feelings—it was odd to have one profound matter altered, almost incidentally, by another. When asked by the Warren Commission whether Michael Paine's return to Irving constituted a reconciliation, Ruth replied, "I can't say that," but today she talks with noticeable cheer about the postassassination years in Irving, when her husband was "back in the family." When Michael is asked whether the calamity drew him and Ruth closer together, he responds, "Oh, yes. Certainly."

They would stay together for seven more years. "Really gave it another try, essentially," says Ruth. Michael set up his own machine shop in town, and at Christmastime 1965 the devoted, if still passionless, couple moved to a new, larger house on Woodleigh Drive. Ruth's routine took her into Dallas, via Dealey Plaza and under the Hertz sign, only occasionally.* Her life was centered in Irving itself, and as her own children reached school age, she became more active outside the home. She helped start a Montessori school in Irving's Bear Creek, a neighborhood settled by ex-slaves and the oldest black community in Dallas County. "I was always pleased," she says with a certain mischief, "that it was the white families who had to bus their children to our school. . . ." Bear Creek, she adds, was really the white person's name for what others simply called West Irving. Her involvement with that community's integrated improvement

---

*This red-neon sign above the Texas School Book Depository has long been part of the assassination's iconography. Its presence at the scene is made slightly stranger by the manipulations, largely unknown, of President Kennedy's father, both for and against John Hertz's Yellow Cab Company in the mid-1920s.

association "enlivened my life quite a lot. I began to have friends that really made sense for me."

An FBI memo from 1965, containing information supplied by the FHA's Dallas Insuring Office, records Ruth's efforts toward integrated housing in the area: The director of the office "was contacted by a leader of the Negro community of Bear Creek near Irving, Texas, who told him they did not want to have anything to do with Ruth Paine and asked if [the director] could keep her away from them." Asked now whether this document is evidence of some personal toxicity arising from Kennedy's murder, and whether activist blacks, already embattled enough, may have been frightened by the idea of associating with her, Ruth responds quite definitely: "I think [the director] was frightened of blacks. That's the way it sounds to me. Because the West Irving Improvement Association, you know, they all knew my history. It was pretty recent history, and one of the people had helped me out with some housekeeping chores when I was overwhelmed, right after the assassination; and we successfully worked with kids in the school district." The WIIA helped effect integration of the town's library and pools, and while it didn't have much impact on housing, Ruth insists that the FHA man's reading of the situation is false: "How typical to say 'The good Negroes don't want to stir things up.' Yeah, he hasn't met them."

During the mid-'60s, Ruth did not sense that she and Michael were being steadily watched by the authorities, but she feels it "certainly is possible" some Dallas police officers took it upon themselves to surveil the couple. She's only mildly surprised to be shown a January 1965 memo, signed by a detective in the

department's Criminal Intelligence Section, listing the auto-
mobiles parked outside 2515 West Fifth. Linnie Mae Randle's
brother, Wesley Frazier, who gave Oswald his ride to work on
November 22, once complained to Ruth that his unwitting part
in the day's events had later hampered his ability to find jobs.
She didn't experience this kind of problem herself but recognized that her peculiar position might affect a small group of
others, such as her old Soviet pen pal, Nina Aparina: "There was
a point when I thought probably she wouldn't want to hear from
me. I thought it could have been frightening."

Some news articles from the weeks just after the assassination have Ruth wondering whether she might need to move
away. Today she recalls moments of uneasiness, but no real
hostility, during the two years she remained on West Fifth
Street. "There were things like my babysitter's mother. She was
wondering what was right for the kids and so on, and went and
talked to her priest. And the priest asked, 'What's your experience with this person? Is this someone that you feel okay about
your kids being with?' So she went with her own experience, al-
though I think she was getting advice from some people that she
shouldn't have anything to do with me."

There were only a couple of hostile calls—a surprise, "considering a lot of people knew about me and knew where I was, and I
did not want an unlisted phone number." The Paines remained
in the book, both on West Fifth and later on Woodleigh. Today
Ruth recognizes an element of denial in the choice to do so: "It
was a way of saying, 'This didn't affect me. I'm going to do what I
would normally do.' And, of course, it *did* affect me, but where I

can do what I normally will do, I'll do it." Yes, she acknowledges, "there are risks in denial," but the strategy, when employed, has generally served her well.* She remained available, not only to newspeople, but to autograph seekers and, as time went on, even those embarked on school projects: "I would like to take off this time from working on my term paper," wrote a student from Kent State University in 1966, "to thank you for your helpful information . . . I find you to be 'one in a million.'"

Staying in the book also made Ruth available to the first wave of assassination conspiracy-theorists. She vividly recalls the earliest of these: Mrs. Shirley Martin of Hominy, Oklahoma, who within months of the crime showed up in Dallas with her four children and dog to trace Oswald's escape route and ask some questions of Mrs. Paine. Upon returning to Oklahoma, Mrs. Martin wrote a near-daily stream of letters to Ruth, who assessed her with shrewdness and sympathy to the FBI's Jim Hosty and Bardwell Odum. "Mrs. Paine characterized Mrs. Martin as a 'bright nut,' explaining that Mrs. Martin has an excellent mind up to a certain point but in her opinion reaches certain conclusions, which may be foregone conclusions, in spite of the evidence." Ruth speaks of her today with evident emotion, as one more curious casualty of the Kennedy assassination: "You have to understand, I think her life came apart. You know any of the further history? I believe her daughter was struck as a pedestrian and killed, and I think she saw it as part of a plot . . . and

---

*When the Secret Service suggested that Robert Oswald get an unpublished number, he declined by saying: "I want to know which way the wind is blowing." Like Ruth, he remains listed even now.

then her marriage fell apart. I think the husband was tired of her having a single notion. So I think she stopped . . . Anyway, I thought it was very sad. She was obsessive about the story."*

At the time of Shirley Martin's first visit, Ruth did not realize that this Oklahoma woman would turn out to be a not-particularly-extreme prototype of the small army of assassination "researchers" that would assemble itself in the decades to come. Many of these would take their inspiration from a man who served his first subpoena to Ruth at the West Irving Montessori school during the week of Martin Luther King's assassination in April 1968. "I remember my stomach turning at that point," says Ruth. According to the summons, Mrs. Paine's presence was required in New Orleans by its district attorney, Jim Garrison, who felt pretty sure she could help him construct the real story of John F. Kennedy's murder.

# Three

Jim Garrison eventually—more or less—settled on the CIA as dark prime mover of the Kennedy assassination. But during his years of pseudoinvestigation, the DA changed and recycled players and plots with such frequency that he seemed to be running, in the minds of those trying to follow him, a sort of reper-

---

*In fact, Mrs. Martin told me in a recent telephone conversation, she continues to study the assassination every day.

tory theatre whose dozen different plays managed to contain the same Jacobean climax.

The most constant elements of his "case"—it is impossible to write about Garrison without the use of such quotation marks—were the man he arrested on March 1, 1967 (International Trade Mart director and noted French-Quarter preservationist, Clay Shaw), and an informant, Perry Russo, who with the help of hypnotism, truth serum, and egomania, helped to finger the accused. And yet, as Patricia Lambert points out in her excellent book *False Witness*, Garrison told various interviewers and audiences, in 1967 alone, that Kennedy's murder had involved, among much else, an abandoned plot to assassinate Fidel Castro; homosexual thrill-killers; neo-Nazis; Russian exiles; the John Birch Society; shooters on the grassy knoll, in front of the car, behind the car, and sticking up from the storm sewer beneath Elm Street.

Lambert once counted herself among the many interested observers who felt that this DA, an elected official in a major American city, must "have *something*." Why else would he be pursuing a matter that the federal government had already investigated so thoroughly? In fact, Garrison had everything and nothing. Public desire to believe that President Kennedy could not have been killed by a single, pouting "lone gunman" was strong enough, when coupled with the DA's willingness to abuse his office, to keep Garrison's fantasy active for years. He would subpoena, question, accuse, and suborn a panoply of oddballs and solid citizens; some, like Clay Shaw, had never even met Oswald, while others, like Ruth Paine, actually had. Whether

Garrison would make Mrs. Paine into a killer or a heroine depended, not on the facts, but on what possibilities she might present once she got to town.

Thomas Bethell, now a conservative Washington journalist, spent some time working for Garrison in the late '60s. The diary he kept, which has become publicly available within the last several years,* is perhaps the chief reality index to the workings of Garrison's office, if not mind. (No one knows for sure whether the district attorney believed any of his scenarios himself.) Bethell recounts a staff meeting that the DA held on Sunday, January 28, 1968, more than two months before Ruth Paine got her subpoena. Vincent Salandria, a Philadelphia lawyer who, like comedian Mort Sahl and author Mark Lane, was occasionally a part of Garrison's operation, addressed the group. Salandria

> started off by telling us that we were in much better shape now than on the occasion of his earlier visit, in July. I had accompanied him around at that time, and I recall he was shown the Shaw file. He looked through it, and was rather rueful about it to me. He admitted to me that there wasn't much there. Now, however, it was a different story, or so he seemed to think . . .
>
> He then started to urge us that the only trouble was

*Bethell fell out with Garrison after realizing that Shaw was being framed. He gave a typescript of his diary to Shaw's lawyer, William Wegmann, after Shaw's trial. Following the attorney's death in 1989, his daughter, Cynthia Wegmann, gave a collection of her father's papers, including the diary, to the National Archives.

we weren't going far enough, and he then started to work himself up into a harangue about Michael and Ruth Paine. "They're agents," he said, "I know they're agents. I've got the proof." He went on at some length about how he had met the Paines, and he produced some quasi-evidence suggesting they were agents etc. Then he told us to go ahead and charge the Paines—"You've got all the evidence you need." He exhorted us to charge some others too, Marina Oswald, and [Allen] Dulles. Don't worry about anything, just go ahead and charge them, "the evidence is THERE!"

Garrison sat next to Salandria through all this, calmly smoking his pipe. Salandria was getting really worked up by this time, and was actually shouting at us. Someone asked him to tell us some of the evidence, and then he pulled out a few card indexes—seemingly a little annoyed at being distracted by such trivia—and then started off on his stuff about troop increases in Vietnam. . . .

One thing is certain: Salandria had met the Paines. He had seen them in Irving, in August of 1965, when Shirley Martin, who already knew him from the nascent network of conspiracy theorists, brought him along on one of her visits to Texas. Three days later Mrs. Martin apologized to Ruth for the lack of any "advance notice" about Salandria. She admitted that he had been "terribly excited" by the encounter, which left him more convinced than before of the Paines' involvement in the assassination.

Almost three years later, on April 7, 1968, a week and a half before Ruth's appearance in New Orleans, Salandria visited her

mother in Ohio. He upset Mrs. Hyde—as she reminded him in a
letter the next day—with "some very serious charges concerning
my daughter and her husband. In effect you have said they are or
were working for the CIA, and as undercover agents were not to
be trusted." Mrs. Hyde had called Ruth after Salandria's visit,
and she now reported to him her daughter's own puzzlement
over "*why* in the world she would consider working for the CIA.
What possible motive could she have? It was obvious that she
could think of none. However, when I said you wanted her to
take a lie detector test, she was willing."

Before leaving for Louisiana, Ruth was called before a criminal district court judge in Dallas County for a very different sort
of legal experience from any she had had with local authorities
at the time of the assassination. She remembers how, this time,
they seemed concerned about the possibility of her "being captured by Louisiana." The judge issued an order noting that "witness will have protection from arrest and service of civil and
criminal processes in connection with matters which arose
before her entrance into the State of Louisiana." The safeguard
might be customary for grand-jury witnesses traveling across
state lines, but it was anything but *pro forma* for someone being
subpoenaed into Garrison's domain.

On $120 of the DA's expense money, Ruth was in and out of
New Orleans so quickly she can't recall for sure whether she
stayed overnight with a Quaker family or came home the same
day. Before spending four hours in front of the grand jury, she
spoke outside the courthouse to reporters, who took note of her
being "chicly dressed in a blue suit with white gloves and white
shoes." Ruth remembers the ensemble having been inspired by

politeness: "I had heard that in the South a lady was defined by the gloves she wore, so I thought, well, I'd better wear gloves."

Despite the already enormous coverage, she had not closely followed Garrison's investigation. The New Orleans *States-Item* reported that, even on the day of her grand-jury appearance, she "clutched a book on teaching methods . . . to pass the time while waiting to testify." She wasn't one of those, she says now, "trying to figure out whether he 'had' anything or not." But some of the notes she kept at the time show her struggling, briefly, to enter Garrison's way of thinking:

---

2530 W. 5                      2534
                                          had children

Wm
    Simmons & Bill Willis

                    Played at the Carousel

                    John Anderson
                        Trumpet player

---

This was the sort of thing Garrison always "had": the fact that two fellows living on Ruth's block had once played music at Jack Ruby's club might, or must, or could be made to, mean something. There was little point in figuring out the implication, since some other coincidence, soldered to some other scenario, would soon render the first "connection" irrelevant. Even so, Garrison never retired any link once it had been made; it went on the shelf, with a hundred other used and spare parts that might yet again be pressed into service.

One of his staffers tried to cannibalize Ruth's old Hallmark calendar for a few parts that might go into the monstrosity the DA's office was trying to build. She remembers him saying, " 'Would you explain these Xs that you have on your date book?' And I said, 'Well, most people keep track of their menstrual periods,' and he *flushed* so red.' He was sorry he'd asked, but as far as I was concerned, better to know than to wonder!"

Vincent Salandria's January tirade against the Paines did not result in any action against Ruth or Michael, but it was not the absence of evidence that compelled Garrison's restraint; only a lack of support from his subordinates deterred him. On that Sunday, according to the Bethell diary, he was

trying to use Salandria to persuade us of a course of action which he wanted to take himself but knew that we would not endorse . . . he was hoping that we might accept it if it came from somebody else, namely Salandria. But the ruse had not worked.

In the end, Garrison did not even summon Michael Paine to appear before his grand jury, and when Ruth arrived in New Orleans, the DA had decided to give her an entirely different function from the one he'd been ready to assign in January. Twelve weeks after hoping to charge her in Kennedy's killing, he decided to make her into a fellow gumshoe, someone who might perform a great patriotic service by coming over to his side with some overlooked piece of information.

After her appearance before the grand jury, Ruth, hungry from a long day of travel and testimony, was brought into Garrison's office with a couple of other people, including a man from *Ramparts* magazine. She recalls:

Garrison had a can of Metrecal. Do you remember Metrecal? Does anyone remember Metrecal? There he was drinking his Metrecal, and I was starving, and nobody was talking about feeding me anything. I'd gotten up at four in the morning or something. And Garrison began explaining, with chalk in hand and a chalkboard, how the CIA was training people out in the parish, out in the swamps, or whatever . . . I was definitely feeling, "I'm surrounded by some very strange people here. What is going on? What is going on here? . . . Can't I go home?"

She remembers that later, talking only to her, Garrison tried "to pull heartstrings: 'We all loved John Kennedy so much, and he's such a loss, and you know . . .' And I'm saying, 'Yes, that's right.' And he said, 'I know you'd want to help in any way you could. Mrs. Paine, *search your memory*. Who did you see with Lee Oswald? What did you see him do with other people?'" Alas, Ruth had almost never seen Oswald with anyone but his family and hers.

Having now twice proved a disappointment to the DA, Ruth returned to New Orleans the following year as a defense witness for Clay Shaw, who finally came to trial in January 1969. She took the stand on Saturday, February 22nd, six years to the day after meeting Lee and Marina Oswald at Everett Glover's party in Dallas.* She had no new information to impart, but she did provide, by way of rebuttal to Perry Russo, the next morning's headline for the *Times-Picayune:* NEVER SAW OSWALD BEARDED —MRS. PAINE. According to the paper, Russo had

> testified that a Leon Oswald, who, along with David W. Ferrie and a Clem Bertrand [Shaw's supposed alias], allegedly plotted to kill the President here in 1963, was dirty and unkempt and needed a shave. But Mrs. Paine said she never saw Lee Harvey Oswald when he wasn't neat and clean.

Garrison himself did not show up for Ruth's testimony; Assistant DA James Alcock made the state's objections and conducted cross-examination. He had a peculiar notion of what constituted hearsay, one that took in utterances Ruth had heard directly, and which Judge Edward Haggerty did nothing to correct. By the time Shaw's lawyer, Irvin Dymond, attempted to question Ruth about her by-now-famous call to Mr. Truly, she was already uncertain about what she would be permitted and not permitted to say:

> Q. What did you do?
> A. I telephoned the Texas School Book Depository and asked whether they were employing at this time, whether they did have an opening.
> Q. To your knowledge, was any appointment made?

*Marina had testified, also for the defense, a day prior to Ruth's appearance. They did not run into each other.

A. Appointment? No. You [meaning Alcock] have got
me confused on how to describe what the man said without
saying what he said.

(Laughter in the courtroom.)

THE BAILIFF: Order! Order!

MR. DYMOND: You can't very well do that.

MR. ALCOCK: That is hearsay.

THE WITNESS: I heard him say it.

Ruth remembers how she "chewed over that all the way home
and for years afterward. You know, this was not hearsay evidence." It was something Truly had said to her directly: "This is
*earwitness* . . . I was confused by their even raising the question.
I was effectively stopped from testifying. . . ."

After she left the courtroom, Ruth met someone from the
League of Women Voters. "I thought, 'Oh, good. Good solid sensible person.' And she said, yes, she's been attending every session, and I said, Well, what does she think? She said, 'Well,
where there's smoke, there's fire.' I thought, Oh, no!" Recalling
the incident, Ruth laughs: "I gave up at that point."

The trial transcript shows some of the same nervous, cooperative gaiety from five years before in the Dallas police station.
Laughter, from both witness and courtroom, is noted more than
once. Ruth even says "Oops!" after mentioning that "Lee was
afraid of losing his job" and then realizing she's stated her own
inference as fact. In *American Grotesque*, his book on the Garrison travesty, James Kirkwood notes that Ruth's entrance "au-
gured a breath of fresh air in an otherwise stale courtroom . . .
She left her audience immeasurably cheered up, not particu-

larly by her testimony, but by her presence." Under the DA's influence, the Criminal Courts Building on Tulane Avenue seethed with mendacity and soundless violence.* But Ruth came to the stand casually wreathed in conscientiousness and good will. However unconvincing to the League of Women Voters lady, she contributed a certain rationality to the proceedings that may, in its way, have helped to speed Shaw's acquittal, which came less than an hour after the jury got the case.

Garrison stopped at nothing. Two days later he had Shaw re-arrested for perjury, in what proved to be a fruitless attempt at imposing double jeopardy. Ruth Paine had been in grave danger from this man, but when asked today if she ever feared arrest and indictment—let alone thought of hiring a lawyer—she says no. Pressed to explain why, she releases some of the laughter that helped purify the air in Judge Haggerty's courtroom: "Pure innocence. You know, I had no idea people could be that crazy." Upon further reflection, she scolds herself for not making more of an effort to comprehend the situation. "*If* I'd thought, I could easily have thought I was vulnerable to that kind of nonsense. But I just never gave it any thought. I was teaching Montessori school, you know; I had other things to do that were more inter-esting and more real." This time she was too naive for even the denial that sometimes served a purpose: "Denial, you have to have some inkling that there's something you're denying. It just seemed a long way away and not anything that was going to get to me."

---

*Garrison contrived a way to show the Zapruder film of the shooting, at that point never seen by the public, again and again to the aghast jurors.

Garrison's fiction was adapted for the movies more than twenty years after everyone who lived outside New Orleans and wasn't a conspiracy buff had forgotten about him. *JFK*, Oliver Stone's variation upon the DA's fantasy—with Kevin Costner as a Jimmy Stewart-like Garrison and Tommy Lee Jones as a mincing version of the hugely dignified Clay Shaw—opened in late 1991. Shot in the rapid-fire style of rock video, a form powerfully suited to suggestion but deliberately unconducive to thought, the film became more familiar than the Warren Report to a new generation of Americans.

"Stone himself says he was telling a story," Ruth argues, "but people don't remember that or don't think about that. It's not announced as pure fiction. And they do things like showing pictures of somebody in a darkroom making changes to a photograph after they say that Oswald said that his head was put on that picture of him with the guns and so on—never saying 'This was done,' but implying it very clearly, and it's that kind of manipulation of truth that offends me."

The director never contacted Mrs. Paine, but the actress playing her did telephone with a few questions. The part had been made very small ("Which was fine!" says Ruth) and the character renamed "Janet"—also fine, since it gives Ruth "the opportunity to say, 'Well, this [movie] is about as true as my name in it.'"* Even the few minutes that "Janet" spends on-screen are inaccurate: She has to separate Lee and Marina when

*Ruth believes that Stone changed her name because, despite her having been an important Warren Commission witness, she probably meets the legal standard for being a private figure. "I suppose I am. Why wouldn't I be? I never ran for office. I haven't published."

they've come to blows, though Ruth "never saw them fight physically. So it was just, I don't know, just garbage." She jokes that
she wouldn't go see it in a theatre because she "wanted to be able
to stop—and go to the bathroom." She eventually viewed it as a
rental on her VCR; the video copy that someone gave her after
that remains on a shelf in her home, still in its plastic shrink-
wrap.

But having given even Lee Harvey Oswald his due in her
words to the Warren Commission, Ruth does not let Oliver
Stone go without a small measure of praise for the way his movie
spurred creation of the federal government's Assassination
Records Review Board, which oversaw the declassification and
release of thousands of documents throughout the 1990s. The
ARRB "did a crackerjack job that needed to be done," she says.
"So, yes, I would say that was a positive thing. I don't think it's
meant that much difference for those who are sure there was a
plot. But still, for a real researcher. . . ."

Much of what the Board released is mind-numbingly pe-
ripheral and generally gets used, not in the interest of greater
meticulousness, but as kindling for ever-higher bonfires of
the conspiracist imagination. In the long run, one would rather
have it available than not, though its appearance hardly justifies
the making of Stone's film, which implies, with cowardly vivid-
ness, that numerous figures in the United States government
conspired to kill the country's President. Before he was buried
with fragments of Oswald's ammunition still in his wrist, Texas
governor John Connolly characterized the production as "evil."
Reminded of this description, Ruth says that she herself "would

say 'without conscience.'" But she allows that evil remains a "perfectly good word."

# Four

At the end of the 1960s, Michael's stepfather, Arthur Young, took another look at the Paines' astrological charts. Ruth remembers him saying, "Oh, you're the one!" It seems she had the planet for independence in the house of partnership—not a signal for smooth marital sailing. "And I thought," she recalls, "'Yeah, I *like* being independent.' But then Michael liked *me* independent, so that doesn't really explain anything." Still, the reading did "help relieve some of that onus, as if [Michael] were the only one who was at fault here, which is never the case when people are breaking up."

Even Texas divorce law now conceded as much, so as the Paines again prepared to part, they did not have to go through the legal charade of "cruelty" accusations. Michael believes a new romantic confidence allowed Ruth to press once more for the divorce. "I have never asked her," he says, "but I thought she had probably experienced sexual love" with a man she'd gotten to know in West Irving. He thinks, "perhaps, that she'd always been disappointed that I hadn't pleased her in that, that I'd withheld myself in a certain sense, in that regard. So I never found fault with her doing that. I've never had any quarrel with Ruth about anything."

By 1970 Michael had passed forty, and Ruth was nearing it. He was about to begin a long odyssey of self-discovery that would take him to North Carolina, back to the Forbeses' New England, in and out of a second marriage. Ruth, too, would return to a more familiar landscape. She departed Irving for Philadelphia in 1971, as soon as she could get Lynn into the sixth grade at Germantown Friends. She herself soon became principal of a Quaker elementary school, Greene Street Friends, an "absolutely charming place" where she had no problem telling people her peculiar history. Candor seemed useful: "When somebody came in at the door and said, 'I want to talk to Mrs. Paine, the one who knew Oswald,' they were prepared. And it did happen there."

She still tends *not* to volunteer her connection to the assassination, but there can always come the moment at which a new acquaintance will stumble on it. Ruth's daughter, now in her early forties, says: "There would be long periods when you wouldn't make reference to it, and there would be settings where it came as a surprise when it *was* mentioned." Ruth suffers less strain when people are aware of the link and she doesn't have to confirm a revelation that's bound to make almost anyone's eyes widen: "I find it helpful to have the information out there, and I don't have to *deliver* it. They can just read, and then they know, and it's generally understood, but I don't have to talk about it."

Ruth's mother had spent the late sixties living alone in Columbus and by 1971 was no longer well. So Mrs. Hyde moved to Philadelphia, too, and shared a house with Ruth and the children; a diagnosis of leukemia soon followed. But it was the health of Ruth's daughter, not Mrs. Hyde's, that made the family's time in Pennsylvania relatively short. Lynn's allergies needed a new, warmer climate, and so in 1975 Ruth moved her two teenaged children to Florida. To get there, they made a three-month journey in a 28-foot sloop. Lynn and Christopher seemed to thrive on the responsibilities and the adventure, meeting new people every time they docked. Asked how she succeeded in getting them out of school for a year, Ruth gives a mischievous, pleased-with-herself smile. "Paper tiger," she pronounces the school authorities.

In fact, her own professional future lay within the public schools of her new home state. For about a year after their arrival on the Gulf Coast, the Paines lived on the boat at the St. Petersburg marina, but in 1976 they moved ashore, and Ruth started work on a master's degree in psychology at the nearby University of South Florida. "I was lucky to get something I really liked; I wasn't sure when I got into it." She joined a gestalt therapy group and began making friends through the local Meeting and the neighborhood Unitarian church.

The family was joined in the airy, three-bedroom apartment by Mrs. Hyde, whose example seemed quietly sustaining as Ruth went about supporting them: "I've watched my mother battling both sex and age as disabilities, to get her bachelor of divinity [in the early 1960s]. But it was looked upon as matter of fact; this is just sometimes what you have to do." Ruth sees her own feminism not as a mid-life acquisition but as a kind of family trust. "My grandmother, my mother, and I have expected to be treated well, and have all earned a living at some point . . . Like civil liberties, you have to keep saying that it's right that women have equal rights and opportunities, and keep making that point. But I've never seen myself as a victim."

At lunchtime one day in February 1978, Ruth received a phone call at the St. Petersburg apartment from two staffers on the House Select Committee on Assassinations (HSCA), which had been formed to reinvestigate the Kennedy and King cases. The committee's origins lay in a new, generalized suspicion of the FBI and CIA: the Watergate scandal, along with the mid-'70s findings of the Church Committee and Rockefeller Commission, had created a public and congressional disposition, stronger than any before, to imagine government involvement in John Kennedy's murder. If not so inventive as Garrison's office, the HSCA proved eager to explore scenarios that linked the Mafia to the CIA, or to Cuban exiles, or all three to one another, in Dealey Plaza.

Despite its initial phone call, the committee never called Ruth Paine to testify—an amazing omission, given her centrality to what it was supposed to be investigating. Today, Ruth reasons with a laugh, "I like to think they read my testimony [to the Warren Commission] and figured they had it, but I really don't know." She admits surprise at not being summoned, though the committee's records, now in the National Archives, show so much sloppiness that anyone looking at them begins to feel the Warren Commission's star witness simply got lost in the shuffle.*

*The committee may also have been too busy pursuing exotica. It managed to locate and take testimony from the Dealey Plaza "Umbrella Man." Visible waving an open umbrella in the Zapruder film, he had been (and remains) the subject of a number of theories: he was firing a poison dart; he was giving

The HSCA prepared summaries of the old FBI reports in Ruth's file—which is to say, summaries of reports that were themselves paraphrases and summaries made by the bureau's agents. The results, compressed and attenuated all at once, resemble badly executed make-work from somebody's summer job: they have Ruth's Russian studies taking place at "Middleburg College," and Wilmer Stratton saying that he and Ruth Hyde "slapped their association" with the Young Friends once they got too old for it. (Stopped?) "Telephone number CA 4-2095" is said to be "identical with the number 224-2090 (area code 614)" belonging to Ruth's father. The summary doesn't say who owned the first number, which is five digits off from the second. And the fifteen-year-old FBI interview of Ruth's mother is boiled into a farrago of meaninglessness:

CAROL ELIZABETH HYDE, mother of Ruth Paine states she knew Marina was at her daughter's and giving birth to a child. States she and her husband discussed active Communist in a "Cooperative Movement" they were involved with in New York, in front of Ruth.

In 1940? In 1960?

The HSCA would conclude that Kennedy had "probably" been shot by more than one gunman. Its acoustical evidence of more

---

the shooters their signal. Before the committee he claimed merely to have been protesting JFK's policies with an object someone had promised him would irritate the President—the World War II symbol of appeasement, the policy Kennedy's father, as Ambassador to Great Britain, had supported.

than three shots, a police radio tape, was later shown, by a rock musician listening to a vinyl insert of the recording published in *Gallery* magazine, to contain crosstalk recorded at least a minute after the assassination. Ruth allows, charitably, that the Committee's conclusions were "a little sloppy . . . It was like the facts didn't add up for them, so they were just going to take this recording that wasn't very clear, and say, well, that proves there were more shots."*

During the bicentennial summer of 1976, while the HSCA was forming and Ruth was getting ready to move into her St. Petersburg apartment, she had received a new round of interview requests and decided, according to a family letter written to Michael, Lyman, and Freddy Paine, that she'd "better read up a bit on what the doubters have been saying over the past 13 years." To that end, she worked through Edward Jay Epstein's *Inquest* and *Counterplot;* Mark Lane's *Rush to Judgment* ("skimmed") and even Jim Garrison's *A Heritage of Stone.*

An assertion in the latter—"It is extraordinary how fearful the government became of national security where information concerning the Paines and their families was concerned"—led Ruth to make two visits to the National Archives during trips between Pennsylvania and Florida. The first archivist she talked to assumed she was doing family genealogy, and in a way she was. She ended up, for instance, delighting in an FBI informant's "glorious description of the activities and interests of Grandpa

---

*A National Academy of Sciences study confirmed the amateur's findings, but in March 2001 the police-radio theory was revived in an article by D. B. Thomas for the British forensics journal *Science and Justice.*

Paine. He came through sounding to me like a spiritual as well as blood descendant of Rob't Treat Paine. . . ."

Ruth was all for full disclosure, and the crux of her family letter was a proposal to Michael:

> This may not come up at all, but if the Congressional investigating committee calls me up I would like to ask that all "protection of my privacy" be waived and all documents made open to the public. The main thing in this area, Michael, is our tax reports, so it would be something you would have to feel appropriate too, for it to be done. Even then, asking that it be done doesn't mean it would be done.

And it wasn't. Ruth's desire for openness here exceeded the government's. She is of course allowed to publish the returns herself, but the Internal Revenue Service isn't going to let anyone look through them—or Oswald's taxes, either—in the National Archives. The IRS remains absolutist about the confidentiality of anyone's return; for years, conspiracy theorists have argued about the "suppression" of the Oswald and Paine tax documents and ascribed it to the intelligence agencies. In fact, those returns are no more suppressed than yours and mine, and the FBI couldn't care less.

Marguerite Oswald liked to call herself "a mother in history," and had no doubts about history's responsibility to her: it needed to put right all the injustice and neglect she'd suffered in prehistory, which is to say life. Ruth saw things in reverse: "I wanted to take care of whatever responsibilities came to me as a result of having known the Oswalds," she says. "One of the very hard things for me is to look back and say I did my level best to honor history and say everything I could that would be helpful. And there's nothing I can do to inform people who choose not to be informed. And that's just going to go on, and I have to kind of protect my feelings from that."

Over the decades she has cooperated with several of the big assassination books: Manchester's *The Death of a President;* Priscilla McMillan's *Marina and Lee;* and Gerald Posner's 1993 *Case Closed* (a welcome corrective to *JFK,* she believes). She has filmed interviews both for documentarians inclined toward the Warren Report and ones convinced of conspiracy, reasoning that, whatever the context, her restatement of the facts, as she remembers them, will be available to a viewer.*

In 1986, she even traveled to England to "testify" in *The Trial of Lee Harvey Oswald,* a five-hour London Weekend TV produc-

---

*Most assassination books do a fast, reductive job of characterizing Ruth Paine. In *Oswald's Tale,* Norman Mailer shows a "serious" woman with "rimless glasses" who with her husband presents "a picture of two exceptionally decent people living under the curse of true gentry: They have been brought up to be so decent to others, so firm and uncompromising about not allowing the greedy little human animal within ever to speak, that one can almost hear strings snapping." At the other extreme, James Kirkwood's book on the Garrison trial overemphasizes Ruth's awkward humor, even discerning a physical resemblance to Carol Burnett. Priscilla McMillan comes closest in *Marina and Lee,* noticing Ruth's "fey" quality, but even she, with so much else to cover in the lives of her title figures, doesn't have time to come fully to terms with Ruth's perplexing affect, the sudden giggles that alternate with a grave and just as suddenly furrowed brow. Mrs. McMillan's book, done with Mation (aired on Showtime in the U.S.) that pitted Vincent Bugliosi (Charles Manson's nemesis) for the prosecution against Gerry Spence in Oswald's posthumous defense. During an amusing, blustery performance—available on videotape to the zealous collector—Spence walks around with a giant photo of Oswald and throws everything he can at Ruth, even the suggestion she might be a KGB agent. He wrings from her the admission that she didn't like Lee very much, and more or less proceeds to treat that as a crime in itself. Bugliosi, by contrast, seems enchanted with his witness. The camera shows him beaming with delight as Ruth gently forbears Spence's assault. The "prosecutor" takes no advantage of several obvious opportunities to object, clearly preferring to let his opponent's aggression backfire. The jury (all Dallas County citizens flown to London) finds Oswald guilty, though a number of them think he may have been part of a conspiracy.

Despite all the missing witnesses and loose legal procedure,

---

rina Oswald's cooperation, was thirteen years in the making. After its publication in 1977, the author remained friends with Ruth Paine, who had been an important source. For some years following, Ruth would hear news of Marina and her family through Mrs. McMillan, until in the early 1980s Marina broke off her relationship with the author. June Oswald, then a young woman, had become convinced, largely through a boyfriend's influence, of both a plot to kill JFK and Mrs. McMillan's participation in a cover-up. One day, during an extended visit from June, Mrs. McMillan returned home to find the young woman and her boyfriend searching through her papers. Marina's embarrassment over this incident, as well as her own eventual conversion to conspiracy theory, ended the friendship. Mrs. McMillan remains grateful to Marina for sticking with her through many delays in the preparation of her book, but has to admit that Marina "goes through people."

the program makes one wonder whether the Warren Commission's findings might have found greater acceptance over the years if its hearings had been conducted on television, and if it had allowed some form of opposing counsel, along with the Commission's own lawyers, to put questions to the witnesses.


Michael and Ruth's amicable parting allowed her to maintain close ties to her in-laws. For decades, her summer travels continued taking her up to Naushon Island and to the two women she considered her mothers-in-law, Mrs. Young and Freddy Paine, each of whom lived on into the late 1990s. "I loved them both so much," says Ruth. Mrs. Young, who in the years after the assassination helped organize the International Peace Academy, was "always a little more formal, I guess, but very open with close family." Ruth's son Chris would eventually move to northern California, where he helped care for her and developed an interest in the cosmic concerns of Arthur Young.

Ruth views them all, including Lyman Paine, as "participants in improving the world," a status she would still aspire to herself, undeterred, after colliding with Lee and Marina Oswald. "I'm not terribly political," she says. "I don't do very much. But I certainly believe in exercising political rights"—among them the distribution of tax-resistance literature at the post office on April 15: "My objection, of course, is to the *proportion* of our money that goes to military expense."

Ruth Paine's own sense of political proportion tends to leave left-wing conspiracy believers suspicious or infuriated. She remains so proud of my country. And that shows up in the letters I have written to my Congress people, when I was saying, "Well, I'm not paying $50 in tax this year because of its association with war and so on." . . . It's wonderful to be in a country where this can happen, you know?

She never liked the shrillness of the anti-Vietnam War movement but admits with laughter that practical considerations limited her activism at the time: "I did," she says, "resist tax payment for a while," after moving from Irving to Philadelphia, "but there I was fully employed as the head of a Quaker school, with a couple of kids and a mom at home, and I just didn't think I had enough left over to do that, too!"

These days the more violent WTO protests leave her cold, and she's not quite prepared to say that the Army's School of the Americas, which she's rallied against at Fort Benning, Georgia, should be shut altogether: "I think it's appropriate for our government to interact with the militaries of other governments—but let's do it in a way that sells our democracy, describes it and *teaches* it, rather than teaching some very doubtful interrogation techniques." At Fort Benning, she says, the demonstrators have "behaved with respect towards townspeople and the military folks at the base," since hostile protest "loses ground in the effort to encourage a peaceful world."

After completing her master's degree, Ruth spent the early and mid-1980s in the Florida Panhandle, working as a psychologist in the Franklin County public schools. Mrs. Hyde had passed

away in '78, and both children had by now left home. Ruth returned to St. Petersburg in 1987 and took a job with the Hillsborough County school system, commuting across the bay into
Tampa, the last city outside Washington that John Kennedy visited—on November 18, 1963—before his swing through Texas.

During this second period in St. Petersburg, Ruth's member-
ship in the city's Quaker Meeting led to the most sustained hu-
manitarian commitment of her life, one with a charged political
background. During the 1980s, she explains, while the Reagan
administration tried to undermine the Sandinista regime in
Nicaragua, "there were some folks in the Meeting here that were
distressed by the embargo. They began a shipping program to
send goods down." Before long a "ProNica" service committee of
the Friends' Southeastern Yearly Meeting declared its commitment in Nicaragua to "community cohesiveness and economic
development, training in non-violent procedures, health, education, agriculture, and women's empowerment issues."

Between July 1990 and the spring of 2000, Ruth made nine
trips to the country. Her report on the last of these for the Pro-
Nica newsletter typifies the youthful, exclamatory manner that
has always been part of her attempts to be helpful—whether at
the Philadelphia Y or the Dallas police station or, now, in the
Nicaraguan countryside:

The first week of the trip I traveled with a group from the
Wisconsin Coordinating Council on Nicaragua (WCCN).
This group has a well-established microcredit loan pro-
gram. I wanted to learn what's involved in making loans

successfully. I learned it's not easy to do it well. A great deal of training, support, research and accounting are required. I went not believing that loans in Nicaragua were made at rates of 2% per MONTH and up (24% per year!). I learned that 2% per month is considered a favorable rate, and loans cost so much because of the management efforts required in order to make [them] successful. Whew!

Articles she's contributed to this newsletter have been word-processed, not banged out on the old portable typewriter that followed her around, and reproduced so many of her personal thoughts, for forty years. She gave the machine away a decade ago. It went, she's pretty sure, to Nicaragua, perhaps in one of the 40-foot shipping containers ProNica used to send down from Florida. The power goes off rather often in Managua, and Ruth thought a manual typewriter might come in handy during blackouts. The same thrifty generosity that once made her send old copies of *Reader's Digest* to a young man in India—and had made Alger Hiss and his Quaker wife, Priscilla, give a more famous typewriter, the Woodstock 230009, to their maid—now assures that, when the lights go out in the Nicaraguan capital, someone is still using the machine on which Lee Harvey Oswald, devoted to the same masters as Hiss, tried to hatch his next-to-last exploit.

Ruth herself was happy to enter the computer era. But the Kennedy assassination had entered it too, as she would soon find out.

# Five

B efore today is over, another hundred postings will have been made to each of the Internet newsgroups devoted to John F. Kennedy's murder. Within the course of a month, *alt.assassination.jfk* and *alt.conspiracy.jfk* will have supplied active participants and "lurkers" with a few thousand theories, rebuttals, interesting bits of minutiae, and repetititve information on the subject. During any visit to the bulletin boards, one can read through "threads" of discussion, message responding to message, on topics such as the following:

> *jet effect rebuttal* [having to do with the physics of the fatal
>     shot to Kennedy's skull]
> *Angle of head shot from grassy knoll*
> *Ruby's Suspicious Phone Calls to Mafia Figures*
> *Re: How About the "Curtain Rod fingerprints"?*
> *HSCA location of wound incorrect*
> *Better diagrams of neck* [having to do with Kennedy's
>     nonlethal throat wound]
> *Did Bobby Kennedy "steal" JFK's brain?*
> *Trail of fragments in lateral X-ray*
> *More Garrison Updates*

If Garrison was a familiar sort of American hustler—Elmer Gantry with subpoena power—the fast, stealthy Web, allowing

Everyman to slip under closed doors and rifle through documents he could never locate in a library, has been a bonanza for what Richard Hofstadter famously called the "paranoid style in American politics." The supposed uncertainties surrounding Kennedy's death have found a natural habitat in the danker precincts of the Web, where everything is, literally, linked.

Beyond the newsgroups are dozens of sites and homepages devoted to the assassination. The "researcher"—a title that long ago replaced "buff"—can download not only Kennedy's autopsy photos but Oswald's, too; can examine reports from the Dallas police department's files; read reams of legal transcript; and view mug shots of myriad figures said to be, somehow, by someone, involved in the crime and the cover-up. But one must go to the newsgroups themselves for the wild, marathon dialectic between those believing in Oswald's exclusive guilt and those insisting on his complete or partial victimization. "Flaming" here extends to charges of being an accessory after the fact in the crime of the century. Claques and feuds and, on occasion, a ululating anti-Semitism cluster around the basic divide between Lone Nutters (LNs) and Conspiracy Theorists (CTs). "So I'm a Lone Nutter!" says Ruth, laughingly appalled by an explanation of the groups. She's heard of them, and has had phone calls from one LN inveterate, but she's never lurked, let alone posted.

John McAdams, a professor of political science at Marquette University, had only "a very, very vague interest" in the assassination until the early 1990s, when Oliver Stone's movie piqued his curiosity and he discovered the newsgroups, which were then, like the Web, in their infancy. He remembers *alt.conspiracy.jfk* as a sort of "free-fire zone." Along with Robert

Harris, owner of a computer-systems business in New Mexico, he decided to begin a "moderated" version that eventually became *alt.assassination.jfk,* the somewhat more civil of the two big Kennedy groups on today's Web. McAdams, though never a CT himself, notes, rather encouragingly, that many LNs are actually converts from that side.*

Helped by two other moderators, he spends about one and a half hours per night sifting through the posts that have arrived, deciding which can go up and which would be better resubmitted by their authors to the unmoderated group. The standards are anything but strict. "The principle," says McAdams, "is any permutation of you-are-wrong we will post. Any permutation of you-are-bad we try to reject." The moderators won't, for instance, let explicit anti-Semitic statements through, but they will allow postings that seem *motivated* by anti-Semitism. "That leads to some tough calls," McAdams says: if somebody blames Mossad [the Israeli intelligence agency] for the assassination, one can guess that anti-Semitism is behind the accusation—but if you can blame the CIA, he argues, why not Mossad?

Posters to both groups will occasionally wander "off topic" to make a point about Monica Lewinsky or the Florida recount, but what Professor McAdams calls the assassination's "mythic status in American popular culture"—his Marquette course on it has a waiting list—assures that participants eventually get

---

*Harris, who fell out with McAdams some time ago, has never moved in that direction. McAdams says that his former colleague believes a final shot was fired from the Elm Street sewer, and that Harris "was a reasonable person until he became convinced that he had just flat solved it."

History                                    155

back on message. Asked what the groups actually accomplish, McAdams, despite the amount of time and trouble he devotes to their operation, takes care not to overstate a case for them:

> The whole activity is unjustifiable if the point is to close the case and prove something to everybody's satisfaction. If it is a hobby, a kind of intellectual inquiry where people are going to learn things—things they will admittedly fit into their preexisting framework for viewing the assassination— then the newsgroups have achieved what would be reason- able for them to achieve.

In fact, the most casual lurker quickly realizes that most posters do not want the case "solved." Their goal is to sustain the imagined mystery's eternal life. McAdams views the LN–CT battles, however seemingly passionate, as a species of Civil War reenactment. There's no telling how long they'll go on; he notes, for example, the recent (unsuccessful) legal efforts of some Lincoln-assassination enthusiasts to exhume, for foren- sic purposes, the body of John Wilkes Booth. The newsgroups are less in the business of spreading the word than repeating writ. They light, not a prairie fire, but a sort of burning circus hoop through which the same gaudy villains and dupes are coaxed to jump, again and again.

Years ago, Ruth Paine observed that, among the letters and calls she got, a geographical pattern emerged: "the farther from Dallas the researcher or newsperson lived, the more likely they were to believe in a plot. So if anyone was across the seas—and people did come from Australia and Europe—they knew there was a plot and there was no telling them otherwise." McAdams finds his own geopolitical split, "a cleavage between the Texas conspiracists and the out-of-state conspiracists," the latter being generally left-wing, the former "sometimes pretty conservative." Overall, he says, there's "a left-wing tinge" to CTs, but lurkers won't fail to notice the presence of an extreme-right subset that sometimes goes into off-topic rages against Bill Clinton.

What the two political wings of conspiracy theory share, according to McAdams, is "a kind of low-level intellectual way of dealing with things. People do want an explanation of what's going on in the world," and they derive both comfort and frustration from feeling that they've got one. He points to the number of posters who identify with Oswald "as somebody who's kind of a victim, somebody who was treated badly by the authorities." The assassin—or "patsy"—is routinely referred to as "Lee" or "Ozzie." On October 18, his birthday is noted, if not exactly celebrated. Had Marguerite Oswald lived long enough to acquire a personal computer, she would be the newsgroups' dowager queen, and posting every night.

Hofstadter delivered his famous lecture on the paranoid style at Oxford in November 1963 and published it, with revisions, one month after release of the Warren Report. His paradigm, which takes in anti-Masonry and Know-Nothingism and the more extreme forms of anti-Communism, has a thoroughgoing rightward tilt, but many of its features can durably accommodate the left-heavy electronic world of assassination "research."

According to Hofstadter, true believers see political conspiracies being "sustained" for decades or generations. (CTs generally insist that Kennedy's killing has been successfully covered up for forty years.) "Time is forever just running out" to expose the plot. (CTs point out that the last important witnesses, like the Paines, are getting old, if they haven't already joined the long list of "mysterious deaths" that followed the assassination.) The "enemy is thought of as being totally evil and totally unappeasable." (The fringiest of CTs talk about an "Entity" that might include not only the old Trilateral-Commission types, but also members of the Assassination Records Review Board.) There is usually a "renegade from the enemy cause" (Pentagon/ CIA liaison-turned-Garrisonite Fletcher Prouty); a "quality of pedantry" to arguments and proofs (the minutiae of ballistics); and, perhaps above all, a sense of impotence and exclusion: "Feeling that they have no access to political bargaining or the making of decisions," writes Hofstadter, "they find their original conception of the world of power as omnipotent, sinister, and malicious fully confirmed. They see only the consequences of power—and this through distorting lenses—and have little chance to observe its actual machinery."

The newsgroup CTs spend much time turning on one another—the message boards are rife with vendetta—and adding more concentric circles to the plot. As McAdams points out, "the classic way in which conspiracists have dealt with contradictory evidence is simply by expanding the nature of the conspiracy." The newsgroups now bristle with insults and accusations against the professor himself, chiefly that "McAss" or

"McClueless" is a tool of the intelligence community: "Multiple posters have claimed that I work for the CIA . . . Harris has accused me of having a whole team of people whom I supposedly direct . . ."

*If I'm not mistaken, the lady that gave Oswald his job at the Texas Unemployment Office, Helen Cunnngham, is a relative of the Paines.* (September 19, 1998, 1:40 p.m.)

*[Michael] Paine appears in the Hughes film, behind the knoll in the parking lot.* (August 31, 1999, 7:54 p.m.)

*I believe Ruth Paine made the entry . . . "LHO purchase of rifle" . . . in March of 1963 and she was lying to protect her FBI informer status.* (May 29, 1999, 3:36 p.m.)

*J. Edgar Hoover suspected both of the Oswald's as being spies. He had Ruth Paine pretend to be a concerned good Samaritan.* (May 10, 1999, 5:45 p.m.)

*Scott Malone reported that when Dallas police searched the home of Ruth Paine after the assassination they found a commercial pornographic film depicting acts of lesbianism.*

(*www.weberman.com,* a now-defunct CT website*)*

As newsgroup subjects, the Paines are hardy perennials. Recycled rumors and charges range from the intensely specific—that Ruth *really* met the teenaged Lee Oswald through the Quakers' 1950s penpal program—to the more vaguely sinister: Michael Paine is "related to 4 directors of United Fruit," according to a poster screen-named lazuli777, who also thinks "it was Ruth Paine's mom who was a friend of [CIA director and Warren Commission member] Allen Dulles's mistress Mary

Bancroft . . . The Paines are all spooked up from the get go." (Actually, it was Michael's mother, Mrs. Young, who knew Mary Bancroft.)

Ruth marvels, almost appreciatively, over how "it's so bizarre, it's so distant," noting that "dear Uncle Cam," whom she knew only as an old man dying of cancer, was probably "pretty unconscious of how the help was being treated" by United Fruit. Some Web suggestions coax gales of laughter from her. For example: "Why is William Hootkins producing British Intelligence movies when Ruth Hyde Paine was his tutor?" asks one CT. "Wonderful!" exclaims Ruth, recalling her one and only Russian student from St. Mark's. (Hootkins is now actually a minor actor best known, at least to cultists, for his role as a space pilot named Red Six in the original *Star Wars*.)

During the waning days of the ARRB, some posters urged that the Paines be summoned before it for questioning, even though the Board had no investigative powers or charge. "What's the harm in trying?" argued one. "They're old now. Who knows what might slip out?" Another disagreed: "Anyone who thinks the Paines' [*sic*] are going to be dragged before a serious inquiry are deluding themselves and wasted [*sic*] their breath. These people will be protected until the day they die." Several months later, somebody else insisted: "Every time I see Ruth Paine in a film, I see a frightened woman. Cagey; smart—but frightened."

One newsgroup legend claims an estrangement between Ruth and her daughter, who supposedly knows the untold "truth" of her mother's involvement in the assassination. But Marin Paine (as Lynn now calls herself) explains the distance in more ordinary mother–daughter terms: "My real problem with being around my mother a lot is that I'm really trying to be a different person than I was when I was a kid . . . I can say she's a nice person and I approve a lot of her values and all that stuff, but [at] just an emotional level she hits trigger buttons that I haven't found the cure for." Marin's allergies tend to act up during concentrated dealings with Ruth.

Professor McAdams, reasonably enough, sees most CTs playing "a kind of parlor game" that American democracy is "robust" enough to put up with. The vast majority of them are not, he says, "going to go move to Montana and stock up on assault rifles. They're not going to learn how to make bombs with fertilizer and fuel oil. They're going to go about their lives . . ." True enough, but one can't say they haven't caused problems for Ruth Paine as she's tried going about hers.

A decade ago, Sue Wheaton, an American aid worker in Central America who had been influenced by the writings of A.J. Weberman—co-author of *Coup d'Etat in America* and, for a while, operator of an enormous website devoted to conspiracy theory—blindsided Ruth with a public denunciation when the two women came together at a monthly ecumenical meeting in Nicaragua. Wheaton managed to convince three or four people Ruth worked with that Mrs. Paine was not to be trusted; they came to wonder whether Ruth's presence in Nicaragua wasn't really a matter of undercover intelligence activity. "I tend to take photographs and try to remember names," Ruth explains. "And that made them extremely nervous."

Ruth cites this as "the *only* place where I have felt damaged by false testimony," and "even then I could understand it, because these were folks who knew some of the terrible things that the CIA was doing in the eighties in Nicaragua." With visible anguish—and no self-pity—she tells the following story:

> A woman who worked with the Witness for Peace . . . said they were instructed: if they can figure out which of this new delegation of people from the north who've come to see what's going on is a CIA plant, leave 'em in Managua. Don't even take that person out to the countryside. Because what they observed was that they'd introduce—it's really so sad [here Ruth begins to cry]—the visitors to community leaders, and then a few weeks later those community leaders would be killed. And they assumed a connection. You know, there's no way I could say to these folks, 'Don't worry.' They *worried*, and they had a reason to.

The reality of *these* "assumed connections" can sensibly be investigated and debated; the shunning of Ruth Paine was a small, irrational piece of cruelty derived from what Hofstadter calls the paranoid's "big leap from the undeniable to the unbelievable."

Part Four    Relics

# One

I first spoke to Ruth Paine late in 1995, shortly before her retirement from the Hillsborough County public schools. I had written her asking if she would do something rather different from cooperating with one more book or article or documentary taking an evidentiary approach to the assassination; I wondered if she would instead talk about herself. I wanted to consider the crime's personal impact on her, and how she had managed to survive association with it. It was not an exaggeration to say that she had been on my mind, in one way or another, for thirty years, perhaps since the night I had read the article titled "Mrs. Oswald's Friend Beset" in the *New York World-Telegram*, my father's paper, when I was twelve years old.

My fiction had often taken the bystanders at American-historical events for its subject matter, but Ruth made it clear that she did not want to be put into a novel—an understandable aversion for someone who had spent decades reiterating the literal truth against fabulists claiming to have discovered the "real" one. She was not even aware of her incidental appearance in several extant works of fiction about the assassination. In 1982, Tommy Thompson, the *Life* writer she met on the day of Kennedy's murder, published an autobiographical novel called *Celebrity*, in which Ruth is depicted as "tall, of stately posture, a brunette in middle years. She projected strength and dignity. Her face had no makeup but her eyes were clear. She probably read Thoreau and baked her own bread." (She would not, however, have referred to Marina as "Lee's little wife" or said that she and Oswald "were learning Russian together.") Walt Brown's *The People v. Lee Harvey Oswald* imagines the accused as having survived his Sunday transfer to the county jail to stand trial, in 1965, in the changed venue of Lubbock; "Ruth," on the stand and risibly out of character, says: "I would have helped Lee Oswald get a job washing and waxing John Connolly's automobile if it would have given him the dignity of work." In Don DeLillo's much-esteemed *Libra* she is a softspoken, almost spectral, figure teaching Lee to drive ("Let's try it in reverse one more time").

I assured Ruth that I had no desire to put her into fiction, as minor character or full-blown protagonist. But the extended essay I had in mind was still not to her liking. She did not—partly out of modesty, partly out of her determination to serve history without belonging to it—see her own story as being of any particular importance. To counter this, I tried an "evidentiary" argument: She had cooperated with investigative books on the assassination in order to help establish the truth, so didn't an essay that explored her life and character "go to the issue of credibility," as a lawyer might put it? Mightn't such a piece serve as the moral ballast for her factual testimony? Her response to this appeal was, in effect: nice try.

And yet, over the next several years, we managed to get acquainted and become friends. She read my books; I began receiving the ProNica newsletter. I saw her when she came to New

York to help care for a niece's new baby, and then in St. Petersburg twice, when a book tour and magazine assignment took me to Florida. Perhaps it was just her politeness, but the door still seemed open a crack, and after a while the assassination, which I'd taken pains not to bring up after my initial communications, began to enter our conversations and letters.

From the start, I liked her a great deal but was never unaware of the gulf between our sensibilities. I could never feel entirely comfortable with her, never shake the sense of myself as a sharp, even cynical, character by comparison. One time, when we talked about our families, I referred to my "caustic" Irish grandmother; I meant the term approvingly, to stand for wit and shrewdness, but I saw Ruth wince a little when I uttered it.

Then, one Sunday afternoon in August 1999, she called and told me that she might, after all, be ready to help with the piece of writing I had proposed more than three years before. Not wanting to sway this bridge we were suddenly crossing, I did not ask what had changed her mind. Many things, no doubt, some of them ineffable. But I got the feeling that John F. Kennedy Jr.'s recent death had been one of them. Months later, when I asked about this, Ruth did not seem eager to address the question, but she didn't deny the possibility. She had always been aware of a similarity between her own small family and Jacqueline Kennedy's ("an older girl and a younger son, very similar in age to mine"), and the young man's fatal accident had strongly affected her.*

---

*Inevitably, suspicions of foul play were expressed on *alt.conspiracy.jfk*.

———————

Ruth Paine's ranch house stands in a pleasant part of southeast St. Petersburg, an older neighborhood where the city's grid loses track of itself and the streets begin to meander; North American egrets sometimes march across the lawns. A backyard mango and grapefruit tree supply fresh fruit to the kitchen off Ruth's uncluttered living and dining rooms. The walls are decorated with floral paintings done by her mother-in-law and some simple unframed maps held in place by push-pins. The overall feeling is plain but hardly austere. Ruth still dislikes eating alone—something she disapproved of in one of her Antioch essays fifty years ago—and during the winter months some older friends join her for a spell of communal living.

As it happens, her house is only a couple of miles from the permanent home of "John F. Kennedy: The Exhibition," a massive display of personal effects from the President and his family. For $13.95 a visitor to the Florida International Museum in downtown St. Pete can "rediscover a thousand days that changed the world" by looking at JFK's doodles, combs, and wallet; Caroline's crayons; one of Jackie's dresses. The exhibit's more than six hundred items were scooped up over the years by the President's personal secretary, Evelyn Lincoln, who passed them on to a young Baltimore collector, Robert White, after he became her friend. In 1998, Kennedy's children declared themselves distinctly displeased by the way Mrs. Lincoln "took advantage of her position."

They succeeded in regaining certain artifacts for the Kennedy Library in Boston, but the St. Petersburg exhibit, supplemented

with memorabilia from the President's November 1963 trip to
nearby Tampa, remains a creepily intimate cornucopia that at-
tracts a substantial flow of visitors—who exit after viewing a wall
of domestic and international newspaper headlines about the
assassination, as well as the uniform worn by one of the police
officers who captured Lee Harvey Oswald in the Texas Theatre.
Emerging from all this Camelotiana onto a sidewalk in St. Petersburg is a slightly surreal experience, fitting, perhaps, for a
city whose other big permanent one-man show is the Salvador
Dali Museum.

"It just raises too much grief," says Ruth, explaining why
she's never gone to see the Kennedy exhibit. "I don't have to do
that." Were she to tour it, she would see the American flag that
flew on the front of JFK's limousine as it entered Dealey Plaza,
an emblem that probably caught Oswald's eye from the sixth-
floor window of the Depository, and which she, too, would have
seen if she had changed her mind and gone downtown that day.
Does she think everything that followed would have been easier,
or harder, if she'd glimpsed the President in Dallas? "Oh, I
think harder," she says, even if harder is difficult to imagine.

When I visit with her in June 2000, this is the sort of question she will answer, hour after hour, for days, speaking softly,
straining to recollect, her voice occasionally breaking. The
plasticity of Ruth's expressions and moods matches the fast
movements of her still-graceful figure. She is peculiarly un-
changed, unaged; she now looks younger than Marina. For
someone grafted to history in such a sad, particular way, she
seems almost disconcertingly in the moment.

Asked whether, at such a remove from the assassination and

after having had to recall it so many times, she isn't perhaps recollecting her recollections rather than the events themselves, her response is definite: "It remains, emotionally, very fresh." During brief breaks in our conversations, she will be in the kitchen, making iced tea or slicing a grapefruit, humming *Für Elise*; and then she will force herself right back to business. When I suggest knocking off for the day, wondering if the point we've reached isn't a good one to stop at, she laughs: "Name it, it's a good point." Still, she would rather do the interviews in large, concentrated blocks, because she can never be sure "how long the cloud will hang on" afterwards. The fewer days we talk, the better.

She will insist, more than once, that the assassination has intruded on her life but not determined it, that her relationships with family and a long career in education have been her true focal points and shaping experiences. The visitor can't help hearing this as the more admirable kind of denial, a substitution of outlook for experience, because if not a cloud directly overhead, the assassination stays forever in the atmosphere. As we try to rig up the VCR so that I can show her clips of old interviews—a conspirators' conference where she's described as part of the plot, and a tape of Marina discussing her current belief in Oswald's complete innocence*—the TV switches for a moment from the video to what's being broadcast: some black-and-white images, it turns out, of John and Jacqueline Kennedy,

---

*Ruth reacts to Marina's assertions, made in 1996, by saying: "I thought she was a better thinker than that."

part of a commercial for a complilation of '6os music hits. To most Americans, the Kennedys are a kind of cultural screen-saver; not a day goes by without our seeing their images. To Ruth, each of these thousands of sightings is a potential trigger of memory, always there for mood and circumstance to squeeze.

She finds the assassination all the more difficult to discuss for being intertwined, still, "with the difficulties in my marriage, and the separation." One understands, without pressing the point, that she has never wholly gotten over Michael, either. No harsh word about him ever escapes her, not even when she's persuaded to discuss the very worst conjunction of the historical and the personal.

In a 1993 interview, for a documentary broadcast during the assassination's thirtieth anniversary, Michael casually told a reporter:

Obviously, [Oswald] liked guns. I went one afternoon to pick him up, went upstairs, and I think the first thing he did, practically, was pick up this photograph of himself—8 by 10—holding his rifle there and some papers. I was a little startled. I suppose he was looking for a big revolution . . .

The program passes over this statement without a follow-up question, though it was arguably the most important evidentiary information to come forth about the assassination in decades. Michael Paine was admitting something he had never told the Warren Commission and never told his wife: that from the very first night he met him, he knew Lee Harvey Oswald had a rifle and had brandished it in one hand while holding two radical newspapers, *The Militant* and *The Worker*, in the other.

Did Michael deliberately withhold this crucial information from the Commission? "No, no," says Ruth; he's "far too honest" for that. She'll admit "he should have brought it up" in 1964 and laughs uneasily about how it would have been "nice" for him to tell *her* before November 22, 1963. But "probably he didn't consider it very important." She claims that, in the several years since someone told her about this interview, she cannot remember ever asking Michael about the matter. "It *didn't* make any difference," she says. "*Could* it have made a difference?" Her voice trails off after asking the question, which is hardly a rhetorical one. To get any further with the subject, she says, "you'd have to ask Michael."

# Two

"I have not been at all successful," says Michael Paine, with a soft, smiling sorrow. "I still feel very incomplete." His hair, at seventy-two, has gone white, but seated in his living room in Boxborough, Massachusetts, not far from the Concord of his Transcendentalist ancestors, he retains his compelling, sonorous voice and straight back. His shelves hold songbooks, volumes on mechanical engineering, and a copy of Robert Richardson's biography *Emerson: The Mind on Fire.* Across the room stands the same large table lamp visible in the television interviews he and

Ruth gave after Oswald's death. Even now, on a summer day in the year 2000, it's hard not to imagine Lee Harvey Oswald, the last one up after watching a movie on television, remembering to turn at least that light off before heading into the front bedroom of the house in Irving.

After his divorce from Ruth, Michael explains, he headed, with his machine-shop equipment, to the John C. Campbell Folk School in the western mountains of North Carolina. He "didn't have an official role" at the school, which since the 1920s had taught weaving and cabinet-making and other rustic arts and whose students grew their own food. While studying dance and singing madrigals, he says, he "just sort of made myself useful." The school fit in with his long-held "daydreams about a more ideal society," but in the three or so years he was there, the institution sputtered: The locals were more interested in studying welding and cosmetology than in learning the Folk School's arcane crafts.

Moving his equipment once again, Michael eventually returned to Massachusetts, first to Cambridge, and then, around 1980, to Boxborough, where he thought he might develop a machine he'd been imagining for decades: "I went to Bell with some ideas about a helicopter that I never discussed or revealed there . . . a very big helicopter. I thought it would be cheap and would enable one to do logging, by cutting up a tree, taking it [right] out of the forest . . . And this place had enough space to make even a model of that. . . ."

The project never succeeded, and Michael drifted into a second marriage with problems "somewhat similar" to those in his first. "I hadn't thought I was courting her. I was going to English dancing in Cambridge, and she lived west of here, so we started car-pooling in, and then I invited her to go canoeing with me. And she wanted to marry after a year of this. And I didn't love *her* yet. I think I've had a problem of not being able to express love when I felt it. And of getting along better with women when I didn't have strong feelings, didn't have that tension. In both cases, that played a role."

Priscilla McMillan says: "I don't think I've ever met anybody more tied in knots than Michael." And yet, when writing *Marina and Lee*, she believed he was "the most perceptive witness" around. "It wasn't what Michael knew frontally," she says. "It was what he perceived," the things he took in with "the corners of his eyes." Of course, she now wonders if "he perceived more than he otherwise would have because he *knew* something." She "was stunned" by what he admitted to the CBS interviewer, about having seen the rifle pictures, in 1993.

When asked to discuss that particular subject, Michael Paine is not at all repressed. It's his explanation that eventually gets tied up in knots, even if the initial narrative of what he remembers from April 2, 1963—the night he went to the Oswalds' second-floor Neely Street apartment to pick them up for dinner in Irving—is, by itself, almost eerily precise:

Yes, right at the stairs my recollection is. There was a little table there, beside the hallway; it went from the front to the back, the hall. The stairway came up the middle of the building. And he first introduced me to Marina, and she was with

her daughter. And then Marina took the little daughter off,
they were trying to get ready to pack up to come with us. And
he picked up this photograph, sitting right there. I suppose
it wouldn't have been if he hadn't expected to meet me
there; perhaps. So we walk back to the couch at the south end
of the building, and he's holding the photograph, I'm taken
a little aback, you know, not knowing, just how to respond to
this. It was unexpected to me to see that. I had expected to
find a theoretician, you know, somebody who was interested
in philosophy or politics or something like that. But he was
obviously, clearly, proud of this picture, and I came to think
it was a true icon he had of himself. . . .

Problems arise with this detailed memory's long slumber
and current implications. What resurrected all this in Michael
Paine's mind thirty years later? The clapboards on the Neely
Street house, he says, which were visible in one of the rifle
photographs shown him by the CBS interviewer. Giving the
word its proper New England pronunciation ("clabbard"),
Michael now goes back again to the early evening of April 2 and
explains to me: "The element of it that I'm most certain about,
that makes me think that I'm not dreaming, is that I happened
to notice, when I was trying to find the address in this strange
part of town, and I was approaching the house, that it had narrow clapboards, which are a bit untypical of Dallas." One was
more likely, he says, to see the "less expensive, wide" ones on
that city's houses, and so the architectural detail remained in
his mind as he entered 214 Neely Street and mounted the stairs.

A minute later, once Oswald showed him the photograph, its background image of the house-covering made Michael surmise that it had been taken just outside:

> I remember sitting on the couch, the picture's in front of me there, and thinking to myself, "will I bring up the subject, inquire about, did he take that picture out here?"*

"MRS. PAINE AND HER HUSBAND HAVE CONTINUALLY INSISTED THEY HAD NO KNOWLEDGE OF SUBJECT'S RIFLE." Being able to take their word on that matter—as this bit of a February 1964 telex from J. Edgar Hoover to two FBI field offices helps to demonstrate—was always central to the government's theory of the case. Just after swearing his oath in front of the Warren Commission on March 17, 1964, Michael was told by Wesley J. Liebeler:

> We particularly want to ask you this afternoon about your knowledge of the possible possession by Lee Harvey Oswald of the weapon that was allegedly used to assassinate the President, or of any other weapon at the time while he had some of his effects stored as we understand it in your garage in Texas.

Shown the actual rifle by the Commissioners, Michael maintained that he could recall *talking* about rifles with Lee, but that he had had no certainty Oswald owned one until the evening

---

*Marina, for all her new insistence upon Oswald's innocence, still affirms that she took the photographs at Oswald's direction, in the Neely Street backyard, just two days before Michael's visit.

of November 22, when they were both inside the Dallas police station:

> I knew he liked rifles because he spoke fondly of them in the Soviet Union although he regretted that he couldn't own a rifle, and I supposed that he still didn't have one so I didn't see a rifle until the night of the 22nd when Marina was shown a rifle in an adjoining glass cubicle between us.

In front of the Commission, he recalled the evening of April 2 as the "most fruitful" of his encounters with Oswald, and "the clearest one" in memory; he told of Lee's gruffness toward his wife before the three of them departed Neely Street with Junie, but never mentioned the photograph, which he today says he was seeing at almost the same moment Oswald was scolding Marina.

He even mentioned the clapboards to the Commission, but only in connection with the *police's* showing him the rifle pictures in November, not with Oswald's display of them seven months before that:

> MR. LIEBELER: Did the FBI or any other investigatory agency of the Government ever show you a picture of the rifle that was supposed to have been used to assassinate the President?
>
> MR. PAINE: They asked me at first, the first night of the assassination if I could locate, identify the place where Lee was standing when he was holding this rifle and some, the picture [later] on the cover of Life.

MR. LIEBELER: Were you able to?

MR. PAINE: I identified the place by the fine clapboard structure of the house.

MR. LIEBELER: By the what?

MR. PAINE: By the small clapboard structure, the house has an unusually small clapboard.

MR. LIEBELER: What did you identify the place as being?

MR. PAINE: The Neely Street address.

So this encounter with the authorities right after Kennedy's murder did *not* bring back the memory of Oswald showing him the photographs; but Michael's exchange with the CBS reporter, thirty years later, supposedly did.

In trying to decide what to believe—or, more exactly, what Michael forgot and when he forgot it—one does well to keep in mind the frequent odd spikes, on any number of subjects, in his 1964 Commission testimony. In a July session held in Dallas, he told Liebeler, "I haven't been thinking about Oswald for a year"—a condition that would have made him almost unique among Americans. He could not remember the year he wed Ruth—"We were married, I think, in 1958, it was the end of the year so maybe it was 1957"—a rather more unusual lapse than forgetting one's anniversary. In the course of explaining how he found the John Birch Society meeting that he attended, out of curiosity, in '63, he made perhaps the first-ever connection between the Birchers and the Unitarians:

There happens to be a member of our choir, a paid soloist who is a John Birch advocate so I have been applying—so I have been telling her, that I wanted to go. I suppose, I don't remember for certain but I suppose she was the one who told me where and when.

While trying to remember points of disagreement between Oswald and Marina on that first night he met them, Michael wonders, almost in the manner of Garrison's Perry Russo, "whether hypnosis would bring it out of me as a tape recorder, or something." Perhaps this speculation, like a later reference to extrasensory perception, was only to be expected from a man exposed to the parapsychological interests of his stepfather, Arthur Young, but one now can't read it without thinking that Michael Paine, while testifying to the Commission, was feeling the breath of a crucial memory he had driven deep below the ground of his consciousness.

He admits to the panel that the subject of Edwin Walker came up at dinner on April 2, though Oswald could hardly, that evening, have let on how his concern with the general was much more than abstract. For the past month he had methodically been planning to kill him.* During the weekend of March 9 he had photographed the alley near Walker's home, on March 12 ordered the $20 rifle he would use, and on March 25 taken delivery of it from Chicago. On April 10, eight days after showing Michael the pictures Marina had taken of him with this new acquisition, he fired once at Walker and grazed the general's hair with a bullet. Later, after the papers carried news of the

*In fact, Oswald's preparations for the Walker shooting were far more meticulous than the ones he would make for assassinating Kennedy.

attempt by an unknown assailant, Oswald's friend George
DeMohrenschildt would ask Lee, only half joking, how come he
had missed.

By contrast, Michael—despite having seen the provocative
picture, and despite having noticed Oswald's peculiar smile
when Walker's name came up at dinner—claims never to have
made the connection. Marina would testify that Lee told her, in
the fall of '63, "Paine knows that I shot him," meaning Walker.
But Michael told the Commission: "I can't see how he would
have thought I knew that."

Nor does Michael see why he should have wondered whether
Lee's blanket roll, which he likely unloaded from Ruth's car in
September and repeatedly later moved, while trying to work in
his garage, might be the rifle he had months before seen in the
picture. "Camping equipment" was his assumption. "You know I
wasn't thinking of a rifle," he told the Commission. "Definitely
that thought never occurred to me." And yet, it *was* the thought
of a rifle—another rifle—that made him think of camping equipment:

MR. LIEBELER. What prompted you to think of that
thought in connection with this particular package?

MR. PAINE. I suppose it was the—I had a .22 when I was
a kid.

MR. LIEBELER. A .22 caliber rifle?

MR. PAINE. Yes; I had two of them. I kept that in better
condition, I mean, this was a rustic looking blanket, it
looked as though it had been kicked around. It was dusty,

and it seemed to me it was wrapped with a twine or something, tied up with a twine. So I thought of, it looked to me
like the kind of blanket I had used for a bed roll on the
ground.

I suppose that is the thought that started me thinking in
the line of camping equipment.

It seems more likely that the thought of his own rifle came to
mind by association, not with a "rustic looking blanket," but
with the rifle he could safely assume to be among Lee Oswald's
possessions on the garage floor. Unaware that Michael had seen
a picture of it, the Commission couldn't explore this more plau-
sible reconstruction. Nonetheless, Robert Oswald, also unaware
of what Michael would later admit, found it odd, back in 1967,
that the Commission "did not seem surprised or puzzled by this
elaborate theory devised to account for the shape of the package."

Today, with her own knowledge of the '93 interview, Priscilla
McMillan, still a resolute LN, would want to ask: "Michael, did
you really think that was camping equipment, having seen the
rifle [photo] in the first place?

Is the 1993 recollection a false memory? Despite what Ruth
Paine says about the assassination's emotional freshness, the
repeated on-demand recollection of any event can dull and
confuse what one recalls. The simple passage of years, of course,
also takes its toll. A number of times during our interview in Au-

gust 2000, Michael Paine, though still an articulate man, would say, "I think I told you," as if recapping something, when he was actually imparting some piece of information for the first time.

But the particularity of what he remembers about his visit to Neely Street argues for the memory's authenticity—just as the trauma of November 22 argues for its having been deliberately or unconsciously suppressed. Even today, Michael's calm, full disclosure seems to involve a denial, within himself, of the revelation's significance.

Thirteen days after the assassination, Ruth told the man from the Senate's Subcommittee on Internal Security that she "could not possibly have guessed" Oswald to be "a person of such violence and hatred." She was telling the truth. But what if she had known about the rifle picture? Michael says it was only after the assassination that he realized his Quaker wife was "so allergic" to guns that "she would have forbidden [Oswald] to have the rifle in the house." Ruth would remark to the Warren Commission about the "mutual honesty, that is exceptional" in her marriage. She was talking, however, about shared *feelings*, not shared information. And it was additional information that she needed in the fall of '63.

When asked by the Commission for Michael's initial impressions of the Oswalds from that April 2 dinner, she had little to offer: "you must understand, that not living together we talked together very little. I am sure he would have given me his impression if we had been having dinner together the next day afterwards. . . ." Indeed, if the two of them *had* dined together, by themselves, on April 3, and Michael had mentioned the photographs, it is reasonable—not some alternate-history fantasy—to believe that Lee Oswald would not have been welcome at 2515 West Fifth Street in October, and that Ruth would not have had the occasion to provide him with the job-hunting tip that put him above Dealey Plaza at 12:30 p.m. on November 22. He would have been left with his addled motive and his $20 means, but he might well have lacked the opportunity. Abraham Zapruder's home movie of a president, not dying but waving, would today be forgotten in his grandchildren's attic.

Ruth acknowledges there was "nothing ordinary about [the] stance" of the man wielding his weapon in that picture she was never told about. And she is willing to ask: "*Could* it"—knowledge of the photo—"have made a difference?" The answer, which has to be yes, is the one truth about the assassination she has not yet fully faced.

Michael concedes that, instead of reading his magazines, he could have paid more attention to the "embassy letter" Ruth tried to show him on November 12. In fact, he should have been generally more alert to the safety of his family that fall. Set aside, for a moment, Ruth's Quaker beliefs: Would *anyone* really want the man in that photograph spending weekends with his wife and children? The question may have crossed Michael's mind. George Stephenson, a Bell engineer who sold him a used car in the fall of '63, would tell FBI agent Hosty

that he recalled MICHAEL PAINE stating "I may have a problem here and I may have gotten myself into something and I better try to get out of it." Mr. STEPHENSON stated that he understood by this statement that MICHAEL PAINE was concerned about having the wife and children of this individual

reside with his wife in view of his pro-Communist statements.

Michael doesn't remember this conversation and doesn't think
the gun was on his mind;* but he did tell the Commission that he
had considered whether Oswald was capable of violence and decided that Lee "wasn't going to stab Ruth or Marina"—a rather
startlingly phrased conclusion. When Mrs. Young, in her December 1963 letter to Ruth, talked of growing almost angry
over what her daughter-in-law's excessive concern for Marina
"might be doing to Michael and your children's future," she,
too, didn't have enough information to consider what Michael
*himself* may have been doing to them all fall.

If one is going to deplore the paranoid style in America's political character—specifically for the ways in which it has twisted
and prolonged the Kennedy assassination's agony—one also
needs to contemplate the nation's transcendent and optimistic
strain, whose evasions have sometimes led it down garden paths
when night was falling. In his reflections upon "The Poet,"
Emerson expressed a sense that "the evils of the world are such
only to the evil eye," to which Melville, in his copy of *Essays: Second Series*, offered this annotative riposte:

What does the man mean? If Mr Emerson travelling in Egypt
should find the plague-spot come out on him—would he
consider that an evil sight or not? And if evil, would his eye

---

*It is worth remembering that many people, after the assassination, recalled
conversations and "sightings" of Oswald that almost certainly never occurred.

be evil because it seemed evil to his eye, or rather, to his
sense using the eye for instrument?

Along with Emerson's blood, Michael Paine carries an inheritance of worldview and sensibility from a host of New England
sages and radicals, not the least of them his father Lyman.
(Michael told the Warren Commission of the "amazing similarity in our natures. I have almost thought there was one person
trying to live in two bodies.") Michael's occasionally antique
diction—he was surely the only Commission witness to use
words like "wayward" and "bothersome"—still allows a visitor to
connect him to the past even before his utopian musings do the
job in earnest.* The thirty-five-year-old man who in the summer and fall of '63 hoped to see a sort of reconciliation between
right and left—perhaps embodied in that paid Bircher soloist at
the Unitarian Church—would later, he explains, read *Walden
Two* and visit experimental communities like Twin Oaks, Vir-
ginia, which offered an interesting labor model: the highest
wages for the least-sought-after jobs. While there, Michael
didn't have to work especially long hours, because he picked
unpopular tasks like cleaning latrines and weaving hammocks:
"A popular job was transplanting strawberries. Now who would
have ever guessed that transplanting strawberries would be a job
in high demand and therefore low-wage? . . . whereas weaving
hammocks was not a favored job, pleasant job, and [therefore]

*When Michael explained to me, in August 2000, why he didn't take any spe-
cial care in shifting Oswald's possessions from one part of the Irving garage
to another, he said he assumed they didn't contain anything valuable or deli-
cate, such as "silver andirons."

a high-wage job." Echoing not only Hamlet but Emerson's above-quoted remarks about evil, Michael declares: "Nothing's unholy but thinking makes it so. Cleaning up a latrine is actually quite a . . . you get a satisfaction from making improvement."*

"It was," writes Lewis Mumford, "the blandness, the sunniness, the mildness, the absence of curses, shadows, shipwrecks in Emerson's philosophy that set Melville against it . . ." And even today, one hardly sinks into paranoia by concluding that, sometimes, a refusal to think the worst of people is precisely what brings it out in them. Insofar as he knew Oswald—they were hardly close—Michael coddled him. He, for instance, refrained from asking Lee about seasonal fluctuations in the Book Depository's hiring patterns, lest he cause the young man undue anxiety. More generally, he told the Warren Commission, he and Ruth "assumed or felt that—if we handled him with a gentle or considerate manner that he wouldn't be a danger to us." He took Oswald to an ACLU meeting in an effort to bring him out of his political isolation, but by that time (October '63), Michael tells me thirty-seven years later, he "had forgotten all about the [rifle] picture."

And yet, when he saw it in April '63, he had had no real problem with Oswald's apparently violent aspirations:

---

*The Twin Oaks wage scheme is very similar to nineteenth-century Fourierism, which Emerson, despite much skepticism, applauded for its spirit: "In a day of small, sour, and fierce schemes, one is admonished and cheered by a project of such friendly aims, and of such bold and generous proportion."

I wasn't offended by it, but I was thinking, 'Oh, that's [got an] awfully remote chance having any value or purpose in our society.' I could see that he wanted to be a guerrilla, in the revolution which should come, or that's what struck me, [that] he wanted to be a guerrilla, showing that he was ready to go, active, able—"Call me"—and I didn't mind that.

If Ruth felt a certain affinity to Jacqueline Kennedy because of the sexes and ages of their children, Michael sympathized with Lee's being saddled by two of his own. Having been impressed by the example of his father, Lyman Paine, Michael tells me:

I grew up feeling that dedicating one's life to trying to make a better world was a very good and valuable thing to do. And raising babies shouldn't interfere too much with it. So I had that feeling with regard to Lee . . . I didn't find fault with the way he spent his life, and Ruth did find fault with him, I think.

Decades earlier, the Warren Commission had asked Michael about the heated argument Lee got into with Frank Krystinik, another Bell Helicopter employee, after the ACLU meeting:

MR. LIEBELER. [Krystinik] didn't indicate that Oswald had threatened any physical violence toward him in connection with the argument, did he?

MR. PAINE. Oh, no; I think Lee knows how to keep his temper, knows how to control himself.

When it came to Lee Harvey Oswald, Ruth's Quaker-grounded beliefs left her positively hard-headed compared to Michael. She knew the embassy letter was a dangerous sign, and she knew her own mind about guns well enough to want them away from her house. Priscilla McMillan, knowing what she now does about the rifle pictures, marvels "that Ruth has rescued a life"—her own—in the face of "all that betrayal" from Lee, from Marina, and even from her husband. But she can't believe that Ruth has come wholly to terms with it.

"What like a bullet can undeceive!" wrote Melville. Perhaps nothing. But not even three rifle shots can penetrate every illusion.

# Three

On the American spiritual landscape, Ruth and Michael Paine may both stand inside the gates of light, away from the paranoid darkness of Conspiracy Theory and Oswald himself, but in Michael one sees more of the self-torturing (and self-regarding) Puritan legacy that remained problematically alive within even its less baleful Emersonian heirs. The New England divines and philosophers always seemed to be approaching—tentatively and the long way round—a place where the Friends had long since arrived and taken a comfortable seat. As Charles M. Woodman put it in *Quakers Find a Way*, a book published during the time Ruth Hyde was discovering the Society of Friends:

Others may work on theories of the atonement all their lives. They may debate among themselves and their various adherents which is right and which is wrong. The Quaker has persistently said in his hours of clearest vision: "Life becomes eternal for me in sacrificial service. This for me is the religion of Jesus."

The light is within one, the connection to the divine already made. An afterlife will be gloriously more of the same.

The St. Petersburg Meeting House, on 19th Avenue not far from the bay, is a simple, shaded brick structure built in 1941, mostly by Joseph T. Taylor, for a Meeting established by former Philadelphians who came down to Florida around the time of World War I. Some of the original furniture, including a pie-crust table made by Taylor, is still there to hold the literature that welcomes newcomers or tells Friends the latest things they need to know about racial profiling and nuclear weapons.

Arriving here on a Sunday morning in June 2000, I find Ruth Paine, the tallest woman in the room, standing on a chair and trying to adjust a ceiling fan before Meeting begins. At 10:30, without warning to a first-time visitor, a hush comes over the room, and the assembled Friends begin their quiet communion with the spirit. After about ten minutes, any children present are released to play outside, but the adults continue in silence for most of an hour. I'm reminded of the Latin Mass of my childhood, during which parishioners got to be alone with their thoughts and rosaries for an hour that made up in holiness what it lacked in oral comprehension.

I know that Ruth, sitting next to me, her eyes closed, is hardly at rest. In 1953, she wrote an essay that described the active peacefulness she experienced at Meeting:

> There I discover and extend a contact with that which I call God. There, occasionally, spontaneous poetry flows through me, without beginning or end; the beauty of life sings in my heart. Sometimes I will see a new direction to my life, or discover an answer to a problem that has been troubling me. In Meeting I reach out from within me to the people around, come to know and understand them, to love them. All these things happen elsewhere, but they happen more in Meeting.

The chief anxiety of the less-involved visitor is that his stomach will growl amidst others' silent meditation. Only a few people rise to break the stillness and share their thoughts. One young man talks charmingly about how bad he was at a recent video game that entailed a lot of zapping and killing—no doubt, he says, because of his "Quaker tendencies." An older man announces that he's been reading a book by Cokie Roberts (daughter of Warren Commission member Hale Boggs) and her husband, Steve, about their long interfaith marriage. Then silence renews itself for a little while, until at 11:30, as if an enchantment has been lifted, eyes open, limbs stretch, and greetings are exchanged. Ruth turns to clasp my hand and say, "Morning, friend."

These people, she tells me, are her family; she wouldn't trade them for anything in the world. And these days they provide her with more week-by-week continuity than her actual family can. She's not yet a grandmother—"I should be! It's high time!"—and her own children have long been off on their own spiritual quests. Chris, out near San Francisco on land belonging to the Youngs, has constructed an experimental plastic house and once described himself to his mother "as a midwife to the Aquarian age." Lynn now calls herself Marin (derived from Tamarin, the name for a guide that came to her in a dream) and believes in a goddess movement that's a part of Wicca. "I sometimes call it Nouveau Witch," says Ruth, "but not in her hearing!" She describes her daughter's belief system as an odd complement to her own: It attempts to recognize "the power of women, and the hidden, the occult—which I consider different from mysticism . . . she's interested in the realities that are unseen." With a certain relief, she notes that Marin doesn't "mess at all with people who want to do spells—like I stay away from plot people!"

Marin herself sees a certain continuity between her present beliefs and the three-sided spiritual inheritance she received from her mother, father, and Arthur Young:

> If you look at the more ecological, feminist, activist end of Wicca . . . certainly that quality is not dissimilar from the particular Quakers that my mother was involved with, who were very much activists . . . and [with Arthur Young] there was an awful lot of paranormal or metaphysical stories of various things unexplained that floated through the family . . . In witchcraft there's really no dogma specified, and I would also say that's true for Unitarianism!

Occasionally, Marin's voice will disappear, like Ruth's, into soft, high laughter, but for all that, and despite the oblique spiritual linkage, a listener becomes more aware of the different manners in which mother and daughter negotiate with the world. Marin is the warier of the two, left that way, perhaps, by a childhood realization that her mother's attempts at reassurance in the days after the assassination—everything was fine, everything was normal—could not, however well-meant, be relied upon. According to her daughter, Ruth behaved, then as well as before the murder, in a way that was consistent with her character: "It would be unlikely that she'd ever project on [Oswald] the things that were true of him, because they're not true of her . . ."

My own imaginative problem, when I glance at Ruth during the Meeting's silent hour, lies in the inability to see her outside a history that I know governs her only in part, and perhaps never less so than now, when her soul is open to so much beyond it. Over the fireplace a wall plaque honoring the founders of the Meeting bears a central admonition from the Quakers' founder, George Fox: MIND THE LIGHT. It sends my thoughts, not to interior illumination, but back to the overhead garage light in Irving, left on that Thursday night in a telltale way that finally told nothing but dimly signalled the path Ruth would be chosen to walk, starting at lunchtime the following day.

At least once each year the CT world rises from its electronic labyrinth to convene a meeting of its own, an in-the-flesh symposium on issues related to the assassination. In the fall of 2000, the JFK Lancer organization (publisher of *Kennedy Assassination Chronicles* magazine) holds its "November in Dallas" conference at a Ramada hotel near Texas Stadium.* The three days of proceedings, a mixture of pseudoscholarly exchange and nostalgia, suggest a cross between annual gatherings of the Modern Language Association and the Trekkies. There are speeches, panels, and exhibits (including one forensic model that has GI Joe-type action figures sitting in for Jack and Jackie in a toy friction-car convertible); a bus tour; an awards banquet; and, for those who can stay on a few days past the last session, until November 22, a "remembrance ceremony" in Dealey Plaza, which now has the feel of a giant diorama or theme park, all of it landmarked in the midst of an otherwise ever-changing Dallas. Tourists gambol and play dead on the grassy knoll and have their pictures taken at the exact point of Elm Street—an X now marks the spot—where the fatal head shot struck.

This year's conference is dedicated to Jean Hill (1931–2000), always known as The Lady in Red for the color of the coat she was wearing in the Zapruder film. The program tells of how she "inspired generations of students" with her eyewitness insistence that she had seen a shot coming from the top of the grassy knoll. (She did not mention this in a television interview given on November 22, 1963, during which she did speak of how the President was looking at a "little dog" riding between himself and the First Lady.) The program also carries a free-verse poem by Bob Cochran, a collector of "first-hand items of JFK, Jack Ruby, and

---

*Participants began assembling on Thursday afternoon, November 16, while far away in New York City, a Robert Treat Paine autograph was being auctioned off by R. M. Smythe & Co.

Lee Harvey Oswald" who attended the same high school in New Orleans that Oswald did, and didn't learn to spell much better than the assassin/patsy: "For violence and deciet combine with hatred and sow the seeds of there own demise . . ."

On Friday morning, the 17th, a panel on "New Research and Updates" gets underway in the Ramada's James Bowie Ballroom, set apart from the Lyndon Baines Johnson Room by a foldable divider. Ian Griggs, "a retired police officer from the U.K." who is "widely published on both sides of the Atlantic and the Internet," rises for an almost heroically irrelevant presentation to fellow researchers. Under the blue conference banner ("Serving the research community, educating a new generation"), he speaks of his stay, this past August, in Helsinki's Hotel Torni, the very place where Lee Harvey Oswald, on his way to defect to the Soviet Union, spent a night in 1959.

"This is not a flophouse," Mr. Griggs tells the audience of about ninety people. "This is not a YMCA." In fact, the Torni has "a James Bond sort of atmosphere to it." Both Herbert Hoover and Alexei Kosygin once stayed there. But why, Mr. Griggs wonders, did Oswald switch to the nearby Klaus Kurki after only one night? Alas, no "smoking gun" turned up in the Finnish capital, but Oswald's time in these two hotels "raises even more suspicions than we felt before," says Mr. Griggs. The speaker is more convinced than ever that Lee was "run" by somebody.

Mr. Griggs, a pleasant older man with a working-class accent, enjoys "this hands-on approach of visiting the actual places, talking to the actual people." Because the Torni changed hands in the early '70s, its old register is gone and we can't know just what room of it Oswald stayed in; so there's only a one-in-ninety-nine chance that Mr. Griggs bedded down within the same four walls. A listener feels pretty sure this is the ultimate thrill the speaker was looking for, but whatever his disappointment, Mr. Griggs pronounces Helsinki a "super place" and recommends it to American vacationers.

*Interesting* is the conference's constant synonym for "pertinent" and "significant." The word can safely be applied to any piece of evidence not gathered or explained by the government. Listening to the theories, one notices the tendency of their proponents to believe that the farther away they get from the moment and place of the assassination itself, the closer they will be to its origin. As in *The X-Files*, "the truth is out there," beyond where anyone has yet looked.

Anna Marie Kuhns-Walko, in an exceptionally rangy performance, manages to touch on how Oswald's half-brother John Pic, while in the military, was always at "bases" that had "intelligence," only minutes after she's remarked upon what would seem to be the much more interesting discovery ("I literally fell off the couch") of some LBJ-suppressed film that she recently bought from an A&E employee who was selling it on Ebay: The footage, she insists, shows that JFK was shot, not by the Stemmons freeway sign, but in the middle of the limo's turn onto Elm Street. Ms. Kuhns-Walko says her health no longer permits her to travel to Washington—not that it really matters: "They won't even answer my faxes and messages at the Archives . . . they've closed the door to me." Beyond that, it would not surprise her that the files there contain misinformation to mislead researchers.* And if you look closely at what seem to be multiple copies of the same document, you'll find they're really different. Debra Conway, the conference's principal organizer, described in the program as "a former retail-marketing executive [who] now works full-time as a JFK researcher and archivist," urges attendees to have a look at some of the stuff Ms. Kuhns-Walko has brought with her: "She's got so many goodies in those little folders over there."

There are moments of pure nostalgia, such as when Otis "Karl" King, a veteran radio newsman who knew Jack Ruby prior to the assassination, gets up to talk about how he was probably the first man on the air with news of "the demise of Camelot." His appearance prompts someone to take a flash picture and somebody else to sigh with the poignancy of it all.

But the conference always gets back to its bloody basics. Larry Hancock brings out the Mafia theory, insisting that John Martino, a member of the Trafficante organization, made a death-bed confession. So did his wife. Like all conspirators, says Hancock, Martino "had the briefing book." The star attraction of the afternoon ballistics panel is Craig Roberts, a "former Marine sniper" with "eighteen confirmed kills" to his name. Apparently part of the right-wing CT minority ("Lieberman and Gore were on the grassy knoll," he jokes), Roberts offers a man's-man approach to the evidence: "Those of you who've fired M-1s know what I'm talking about." The bullets found on the ground by Officer Tippit, the Dallas policeman Oswald is

*During an afternoon session on "Intelligence Connections," a panelist named Gregory Burnham says he thinks he sees a couple of agents monitoring the proceedings from the back of the room.

supposed to have shot, could not, he says, have fit the pistol Lee had when captured at the Texas Theatre, and Roberts says even *he* couldn't have made the kill shot from the sixth-floor window of the Depository. ("That dog won't hunt. When you shoot people, it ain't shootin' deer.") While he has "some problems" with the storm-sewer theory, he does believe there was "a triangulation of fire" in the Plaza.

As at any MLA convention, "November in Dallas" showcases new work on both major and minor figures. Ruth and Michael Paine are decidedly major, a sort of specialty unto themselves, like the Brownings, or Sylvia Plath and Ted Hughes.* This year Florida attorney Carol Hewett is prepared to show why the Paines are "not as benign and innocent as the Warren Commission would have us believe."

Nor is Hewett so friendly as she appears, with her short frosted-blonde hair and small-businesswoman's manner. She runs a video of Michael's 1963 television interview, noting his suspicious, supposed resemblance to Lee Harvey Oswald in both looks and manner (he "licks his lips," just like Lee). She holds out hope of an even better Paine–Dulles connection than the one always made between Michael's mother and CIA Director Allen Dulles's mistress, Mary Bancroft: Hewett now has a genealogist trying to see if there's a link between *John Foster*

---

*Kathy Kay, one of Jack Ruby's strippers, would be minor: Born in London in 1936 and originally named Lilian Helen Harvey, she has been studied "at length for the past eight years" by Ian Griggs, whose exhibit devoted to her includes "eight photographs showing Kathy Kay performing at the Carousel Club [that] were suppressed by the Warren Commission on the grounds of 'questionable taste and negligible relevance.' "

Dulles's wife, who was an Avery, and William Avery Hyde, father to Ruth Avery Hyde Paine.

Ruth "professes to be a Quaker," says Hewett, though her only known act of charity seems to have been taking in Marina. "This woman did not donate clothes to the Goodwill, did not take in stray animals." The audience needs to know that "there's still a lot more work to be done" on the Paines, and that Ruth was *really* in Fort Worth at Bell Helicopter with Michael on the morning of the assassination. "Why this was covered up by the FBI is a mystery."

Ruth Paine has never met or spoken with Carol Hewett, but she did once give an interview to Nancy Wertz, another specialist on her and Michael. At JFK Lancer's 1998 conference, while on a panel with Carol Hewett, Wertz referred to the Paines as "the couple we all love to hate." Nonetheless, in the spirit of the season, she sometimes sends Ruth a Christmas card.

# Four

O nce out of Dealey Plaza, any visitor to Dallas who takes the assassination bus tour will find himself mostly a pilgrim among ruins. Jack Ruby's Carousel Club is gone, and his old apartment gutted. The Texas Theatre, where Oswald was captured, has closed. But 214 Neely Street, with its narrow clapboards, remains standing, a kind of seedy totem to the durability of the capitalist system Oswald imagined he was helping to erase from the world. As the *Dallas Morning News* reported in November 2000, the "duplex is still a functioning residence. Judith Wilson, the downstairs tenant, charges visitors $5 to borrow a toy rifle and pose in the back yard."

The tour bus doesn't go out to Irving, a suburban city now exponentially larger than it was during the Paines' time, but anybody travelling on his own to its older parts will find Ruth and Michael's neighborhood little changed. A comparison of the street directories for '63 and '98 shows names like Butler and Goodwin being replaced by Cortez and Pena, but the new ones have come to West Fifth in search of the same suburban contentment as the old, no doubt quickly feeling more at home than the Paines ever did inside number 2515. The sidewalks are perhaps more cracked and the lawns a trifle less mown than they were in '63, but as the late afternoon light falls on a warm autumn day, the street remains a pleasant, viable place. Walking along, one still hears the soft whistles of freight trains headed to and from the Triple Underpass in Dealey Plaza.

One reporter visiting number 2515 a year after the assassination described "a home where a great murder is upon it like dust that can never be swept away." Today, the only thing a visitor notices atop the old Paine place is a small satellite dish, perched like a magpie and signifying how much less likely Ruth would have been to remain in the house after November '63 if she'd had to endure the media attention that a later age could pay.

Then as now, children's toys lie close to the house's front door, and when I show up in November 2000, the current resident patiently takes me through an interior that seems almost as

mothballed as Dealey Plaza: the same knotty-pine kitchen cabi-
nets, the same light fixture over the same two-compartment
sink in which Ruth noticed Oswald's instant-coffee cup. Beyond
the backyard window I'm pretty sure I see the same heavy poles
of the clothesline upon which Marina was hanging laundry when
Ruth came out with news from the television.

The present occupant says he learned of the house's history
only at the real-estate closing, though since then he's seen the
place mentioned on television, and a couple of times has noticed drivers slowing down to take a picture of it. The structure's
most crucial historical element, the garage, has new doors on its
front and inside. One now goes into it from the living room,
since the dining area where Lee and Marina and Ruth ate dinner
on November 21 has been converted into an additional bedroom. But the garage is still used for household items instead of
a car, and I would be almost unsurprised to see the children's
blocks, freshly varnished by Ruth that night, on a work table
near some lawn furniture.*

Easiest of all to imagine in here is Oswald, extracting and
rewrapping the contents of the blanket as quietly as he can, listening to make sure neither Ruth nor Marina has left the bedroom for the living room where, with just a wall between it and
the garage, they could hear him at his task. Once the job is finished, he hastens back into the house beyond the wall, too nervous to remember the light switch.

---

*Ruth thinks she probably gave the blocks away to a pre-school, around the
time of her departure from Irving.

---

Toward this sort of inadvertency, as well as chance, the CT worldview has near-zero tolerance. In 1968, as he flung accusations and married cause to effect, Garrison's Vincent Salandria was vainly urged by Ruth's mother to make room for coincidence inside his mind—"and fate, if you can."

Those willing to see the operation of such forces within the world might now turn their minds back to Fort Worth on the morning of the assassination. The Kennedys had the night before arrived at their hotel, too worn out from a day of campaigning to take much notice of the paintings—the Eakins, the Monet, the Van Gogh—that the city's small art establishment had hung in their suite. Only upon waking did the First Lady realize just what was here. Finding a two-page catalog of the exhibit, she showed it to the President, who suggested they telephone one of the five people credited at the bottom. They picked the first name, Mrs. J. Lee Johnson III, daughter of the newspaper publisher and art collector Amon Carter. Thus, as William Manchester says in his account of the incident in *The Death of a President*, Mrs. Johnson, home that day taking care of a sick child, "became the surprised recipient of John Kennedy's last telephone call."

Years later, in *Oswald's Tale*, Norman Mailer quoted Manchester's account and added his own delighted commentary upon fate:

Mrs. J. Lee Johnson III! One has to observe that her married name bears the first initial of J. Edgar Hoover, has Lee in the middle, and ends with the last name of the President who will succeed Jack Kennedy. (As a bonus, her maiden name is Carter.) Perhaps the cosmos likes to strew coincidences around the rim of the funnel into which large events are converging.

Mailer actually didn't know the half. In the fall of 2000, when I spoke with Ruth (yes) Carter Stevenson—later life has supplied her with another nearly presidential name—she remembered the morning of November 22 very well: "I nearly fell through the telephone." The exhibit, she explains, started with:

a press photographer, Owen Davis, I think his name was, Owen something, who thought up the idea. Then Sam Cantey took it over, and I got in the act, and I went around picking up works of art all over the place to take down there. And from my own house and from the Basses and from the Wein-ers and odds and ends and places. . . .

Did she herself help set things up at the Hotel Texas? I ask. "Hell, yes, I was over there! They'd just washed all the carpets and we were all in stockinged feet." Mrs. Stevenson was on fa-miliar ground; her brother and sister-in-law, during the first weeks of their marriage, while waiting for their own house to be ready, had lived in the suite now being prepared for the Kennedys. This same couple, later on, had employed a local woman, Mrs. Marguerite Oswald, as a babysitter, until they de-cided she was too odd a character and, as Mrs. Stevenson puts it, "discontinued" her. At the time of the assassination, Mrs. Oswald, who had angrily failed at various of retail jobs, was working as a practical nurse.

On November 21, a Secret Serviceman who looked at the haul of art being brought into the hotel remarked to Mrs. Stevenson: "It's sort of valuable, isn't it?" She recalls telling him, "Yes, but we don't worry about things like that here in Fort Worth. [The paintings] were probably covered with blankets." She had no intention of attending the President's Friday-morning breakfast speech—"I didn't vote for Mr. Kennedy"—but she agreed, at the Secret Serviceman's suggestion, to stand at the hotel's elevator door so that the President might thank her personally on his way down to the ballroom.

In the event, her daughter got sick and she accepted JFK's thanks over the telephone. She remembers talking to Jackie, who came on second, with particular clarity:

she got on the phone, too. What I didn't know until later is that we'd hung all the French paintings in the bedroom where the king-size bed was, and then had Remingtons and Russells in this smaller bedroom, which we presumed he would sleep in. Well, then they switched on us, so he was sleeping in the room with the Monet and the Van Gogh, and she was in the other bed. I thought it was rather strange when she called, when she got on the phone, and she said, "It was so late and we were so tired, I didn't realize it was real art," which took me back a little bit, and I thought, "Here, girl, you've borrowed everything from the Boston Museum

you can get your hands on for the White House, and you
don't recognize a Van Gogh or a Monet?" . . . I didn't find
this out [about the switch] until much, much later.*

I had called Mrs. Stevenson to get hold of the catalog, which
she helped obtain for me from the Amon Carter Museum
archives, as well as to ask if the President had requested that she
convey his thanks to the other four people involved in assembling the exhibit. Yes, he did, and she proceeded to do that, sick
daughter and all, right away.

Raymond Entenmann, then director of the Fort Worth Art
Center, remembers quite clearly the call he got from Ruth Johnson. In fact, says his wife, Ilse, the whole story of the exhibit is
"something we hold in our memory"—the worst part of it being
how news of the assassination reached Ray later in the day. He
remembers hearing it with "two of the directors of the museum," each a pillar of the conservative city: "They were almost
impossible. They were almost cheering."

Still active as a landscape architect and designer of interiors,
Mr. Entenmann laughed when telling me, last fall, about the
paintings he helped round up in '63, a time when Fort Worth's
cultural institutions were rather more modest than they are
today: "Let me tell you, they were not all from the museum!"
More gravely, he volunteered the peculiar coincidence of how
he'd also been at the Hotel Texas on January 20, 1961, to meet
with an art dealer. That day he left the hotel with a trunkful of

---

*Two small corrections to Mrs. Stevenson's memory: the catalog shows a Rus-
sell but no Remington, and the press photographer's name was Owen Day.

paintings and heard Kennedy's inaugural address on the radio of the limousine he was in. "We even heard Robert Frost, and were sitting there absolutely enthralled." He now expresses wonder over the parallels—the two trunkloads of paintings, the Hotel Texas, the first day of the administration and the second-to-last.

But he knows I've called about an even odder coincidence. I've tracked him down because of one line in the report of an FBI interview he gave in 1964. According to the report, the subject and his wife spent election night 1960 "in the home of the PAINES," their old friends from Philadelphia, also newly transplanted to Texas. Yes, the Entenmanns both recall, aside from Ruth and Michael they were probably the only Democratic voters at the little gathering inside 2515 West Fifth.

Once I'd seen the FBI report identifying his position at the Fort Worth Museum of Art, I had surmised that Raymond Entenmann must have had a hand in the hotel art exhibit, and sure enough, his name was at the bottom of the little catalog. Which means that John F. Kennedy placed his last telephone call, in part, to thank a man who had spent the night of his election to the presidency inside a house that would contain the gun that killed him.

The assassination "kind of severed" the Entenmanns' relationship with the Paines, Ray Entenmann tells me. "I don't think we saw them at all after . . . I think we felt it was embarrassing"—that is, embarrassing for Ruth and Michael. Even with their own personal connection to the President's last day, he and Ilse didn't want to be two more people asking the Paines about Oswald, and about how they were bearing up.

Two weeks after speaking to both the Entenmanns, I call Ruth Paine and tell her about this particular coincidence, whose possibility had never occurred to her. Only after a long pause in the conversation do I realize that she is crying. I quickly apologize, ashamed of the pleasure I was taking in my detective work and expecting her to share, without having stopped to think of how this might be just the thing to drag her emotions about the assassination, yet again, months after our long interviews, to the surface. No, she says, it's okay; she's glad to know of this little cosmic conjunction. We go on to talk about Goethe's idea that the tree of life stands greener than any thought, of how fate's plots can be more intricate than even those deduced by the CTs. She tells me, yes, this is the sort of story I should include in what I write.

And she asks if I can give her the Entenmanns' address.

Ruth's own address and telephone are still listed in the book: "I want my friends to be able to find me." Only rarely has her availability enabled someone's mischief or malice. Several years ago, she says, a caller left a message on her machine: "the implication was 'we know that you were involved in killing Kennedy,'" and the message was supplemented by an announcement that harm would soon be coming to the current President. "I called the Secret Service," Ruth explains, "and said, 'I have this tape, somebody suggesting that there was a threat to the President.' Well, they weren't very interested, and I said, 'Well, look up my name in your database.'" Laughing at the recollection, she finishes the story: "They found it! They said, 'We'll be right over!' I said, 'Well, you know, I could mail this to you,' and they said, 'No, no, no, we'll come and get it!' " And they did.

Today, the metal file box with the most personal papers from her early life, still bearing its stickered identification as Warren Commission Exhibit No. 458, sits on the floor of her bedroom closet along with a few cartons of published material relating to the assassination. So far, she says, her children haven't shown much interest in the material.* The closet also houses a small box with some of Ruth's FBI files, ordered not too many years ago, partly in the (vain) hope of finding a more current address for Nina Aparina, her old Soviet pen pal.

Another FBI contact of sorts occurred only a few years ago, when Ruth had a reunion with Agent Hosty, long since retired and now the author of a memoir called *Assignment: Oswald.* "He was doing one of those book signings in Tampa, and he called me and suggested I come over, so I did, and we had a nice visit"— even if she couldn't say she agreed with Hosty's current sugges- tion that Marina, back in '63, may have been "a KGB-planted sleeper agent."†

These days, since the end of his second marriage and despite the deaths of his parents, Ruth sees more of Michael Paine than she did for many years. They even toured China together in Oc- tober 2000 and, after that, made plans for Michael to come

---

*Her daughter, Marin, is nonetheless interested in the mythic implications of JFK's murder, for both her own life and the general culture's: "Some- times," she tells me, "I wonder if there's a significance that I'm living two miles away from the non-New York house of Caroline Kennedy...."

†Whether she was or wasn't, Hosty still believes that Oswald performed the assassination on his own, "acting independently of his wife."

down for the first time to St. Petersburg, with movies taken on the trip. Ruth may have traveled some distance from her childhood in a household where becoming angry was considered a defeat, but she still seems able to accommodate Michael's now-admitted foreknowledge of the rifle—a source of fury, one would imagine, to almost anyone else—on some ordinary ex-marital ledger of resentments and pardons.

If she could speak with Oswald himself today, in a sort of afterlife, would she, I ask, be able to express anger toward *him*?

No, but she wouldn't be suppressing it, either: "I don't think I'd feel it at that point. The anger was immediate. The anger was over the loss of Kennedy, and feeling that the gun had been there in the garage." And while it might be interesting to know "why Kennedy in particular, or why he took this course that was so harmful to his family," she would most want to ask a "larger" question, one that's still mindful of the light, wherever God chooses to shine it: "Where are you now," she would ask Lee, "in your learning, and your understanding of life?"

Forty years later, she remains "curious, curious about him."


The Hallmark datebook—*February 22: Everett's?*—rests on a shelf of the Friends Library at Swarthmore. Marina's Russian book of household hints, whose yellowing pages once hid the Walker letter, sits in the National Archives, not far from the blanket that wrapped Lee's rifle. Once a dingy thing to be stepped over or thoughtlessly shifted from one spot on the garage floor to another, the blanket is now preserved as carefully as Jackie Kennedy's bloody clothes, in heavy plastic and stiff cardboard. Its green and brown stripes chase each other in a Mondrian pattern, their occasional blendings making the cloth look oddly like camouflage, which in its way it once was. The Archives has procedures for fending off the morbidly curious, but less secure institutions are prey to the relic-seeking impulse that may be one of the few commonalities across the LN/CT divide. Marguerite Oswald's handwritten denunciations of Ruth Paine survive in her set of the Warren Report's appendices at the Texas Christian University Library in Fort Worth, but someone has made off with Marguerite's copy of the Report itself.

All these things must finally oxidize and decay, but one object connected to the case has stayed alive and even grown, beyond the Warren Commission's measuring tapes and rulers: the oak tree on the lawn at 2515 West Fifth. Today it stands with a thicker trunk and casts noticeably more shade than it did on the late Thursday afternoon, November 21, 1963, when Ruth Paine saw Lee Oswald standing under it, with his wife and child.

Grateful acknowledgment is made to:

Ruth Hyde Paine for permission to quote from private correspondence and personal writings.

The Friends Historical Library of Swarthmore College for permission to quote from the correspondence of Ruth Hyde Paine from the Ruth Hyde Paine/Marina Oswald Papers, RG5/109, Friends Historical Library of Swarthmore College.

Michael Ralph Paine and the estate of Ruth Forbes Paine Young for permission to quote from the letters of Mrs. Ruth Young.

Mr. Thomas Bethell for permission to quote his diary, now in the National Archives.

The estate of Jessamyn West for permission to quote Miss West's letters to Ruth Paine.

Priscilla Johnson McMillan for permission to quote from her correspondence with Ruth Paine.

Mrs. Shirley Lester for permission to quote her (Shirley Martin's) letter to Ruth Paine.

# About the Author

Thomas Mallon's books include the novels *Henry and Clara*, *Two Moons*, *Dewey Defeats Truman*, and *Aurora 7*, as well as a collection of essays, *In Fact*. His work has appeared in *The New Yorker*, *The New York Times Magazine*, *The American Scholar*, and *GQ*. He has been the recipient of Rockefeller and Guggenheim fellowships, and in 1998 he received the National Book Critics Circle award for reviewing. He lives in Westport, Connecticut.